DURHAM QUILTING

DURHAM QUILTING

Brenda Marchbank

Dryad Press Ltd, London

Acknowledgement

I would like to thank my family, especially my daughter Caroline who has been so helpful over the months taken to produce this book; also Frances Williams for all her kind help; Chris Williams of *Cobra*; The Shipley Art Gallery; Beamish Museum; Louise Hamer, curator of The Embroiderers' Guild; The Post Office Archives; The Victoria and Albert Museum; Margaret Swain; Mr A. Graham of The House of Fraser; Quarry Bank Mill, Styal; Mike Rainbird who took some photographs and Dave Russell who printed the photographs; also all who loaned work to photograph, namely, Doreen Soulsby, Mrs Crosby, Ann Hayes, Wyn Bacon, Sue Fielding, Mrs Pickering, Joan Armstrong, Margaret Watson, Pamela Allen, Lyndon Say, Ann Kinnement, Sheila Corfe, Sandra Felce, Marian Bowman, Eileen O'Hanlon, Evelyn Fox, Kathleen Brown, Mrs Graham and Sylvia McLoughry. Many thanks also go the people who have been kind enough to talk with me, giving of their time, knowledge and information.

ISBN 0 8521 9737 3

Typeset by Servis Filmsetting Ltd, Manchester
and printed in Great Britain by
The Bath Press Ltd
Bath
for the publishers
Dryad Press Ltd
8 Cavendish Square
London W1M 0AJ

British Library Cataloguing-in-Publication Data
Marchbank, Brenda
    Durham quilting.
    1. Quilting. Manuals
    I. Title
    746.46

    ISBN 0-85219-737-3

Contents

Introduction

County Durham in the north-east of England covered an area from the River Tees to the River Tyne until 1971, when the counties were re-organised for administrative purposes. At that time boundaries were altered radically and Durham became a much smaller, largely rural county. The large towns of Gateshead, Sunderland and Washington were taken out of its jurisdiction to make the new county of Tyne and Wear – these towns lying between those two rivers. This dramatically reduced the population of County Durham. On the southern edge are the towns of Darlington and Stockton on Tees, the latter with a population of 49,709 in 1891 and 86,699 in 1981. On the west is the Pennine range and such small towns as Barnard Castle, Bishop Auckland and Leadgate. More centrally, there is Durham City (population 1891: 14,863 and 1981: 38,105), while to the east is Hartlepool (1891: 21,288 and 1981: 91,749).

Durham quilting originated long before the counties were altered, and quilts were made in rural areas as well as in the large towns later taken to form the new county of Tyne and Wear. Sunderland, which I believe is the largest town in the country (1891: 131,686 and 1981: 201,008) and Gateshead (1891: 85,692 and 1981: 91,429) produced a great number of quilts.

Durham quilting has great similarities to that of its neighbouring county, Northumberland, and the two styles are so closely linked and interchanged that they are known collectively as North Country quilts. Certain patterns, such as feathering, are common to both, but there were sometimes small pockets of communities which used their own distinctive designs, differing slightly from those of neighbouring villages.

Through the study of quilts one can learn much about the social and economic conditions and changes of the area. The industrial revolution led to the great boom in shipbuilding and coal-mining. There was also lead-mining on the eastern side of the Pennines, and the name of the town of Leadgate probably indicates its involvement with the industry. Lead-mining is no longer an active industry, and coal-mining and shipbuilding have been steadily cut back. This has meant a decline in communities and the escalation of financial problems which people have had to face. Until the early twentieth century this encouraged women in both country and town to supplement the family income by means of quilting.

The decline in quilting accelerated during and after the First World War as women found more profitable work. In the depression of the 1930s the government tried to encourage greater involvement in the craft by sending fabric to the North-East for use by the quilters to enable women in the area to supplement the lowered incomes. The craft's final demise occurred during the Second World War, brought about by the rationing of textiles, and the full employment of women in more lucratively paid jobs. The slump of recent years has had little direct effect on the craft which had almost disappeared, but there is a small resurgence of interest, though this is not usually impelled by thrift as in the past.

The work of quilting is so slow and painstaking that in these times of cheap mass production it is no longer financially practical. There are a few people quilting at the present time but usually as a craft hobby and in this context it is

being encouraged in some further education classes to keep alive the skills and designs of the area.

This book shows that traditional Durham methods can be used for contemporary work alongside the ever-popular traditional quilting. Encouragement is also given to designing small or large articles for oneself.

Fig. 1 *White quilt*

I
HISTORY

The making of padded articles for warmth or protection has a long history. People soon learned that three layers – top, middle and back – when held together met this need. As we see in our modern duvet, the thicker the pocket of air trapped, the warmer the article. When these three layers are stitched together they are given the general name of *wadded quilting*, a method used in Durham quilts.

A second type of quilting is *corded quilting*, sometimes called Italian quilting, which needs only two layers of fabric stitched with parallel lines which are then threaded through with cord or wool. The third type of quilting is *trapunto*, sometimes called stuffed quilting, in which stitching through two layers of fabric follows a design which is then padded or stuffed through the back layer.

Beautiful quilting has been made for many centuries, but the work of the seventeenth century is of particular interest, as at that time quilting was fashionable, as well as being worn for warmth. Gentlemen's waistcoats, ladies' long petticoats and bed coverlets can be seen in a number of museums: the Victoria & Albert in London, the Bowes Museum Bishop in Auckland, Co. Durham, the Beamish Museum in Beamish, Co. Durham, the Castle Museum in York and the Laing Art Gallery in Newcastle-upon-Tyne are just a few. The Embroiderers' Guild have in their collection four seventeenth-century men's quilted jackets. Other examples may be seen up and down the country.

The invention of the domestic sewing machine and the improvements made to it between the years 1845 and 1854, was a great help to women. In 1858 the Singer Machine Company brought out a lightweight family machine, and in 1865 another more substantial one. Not surprisingly, it sold over 4 million machines during the 20 years it was manufactured.

At the end of the eighteenth and beginning of the nineteenth century the fashion for quilted clothing began to die. However, quilts had been made professionally since the 1760s, and continued to be made by miners' widows from small villages, whose husbands had either been injured or killed in mining accidents. It seems that men, too, were sometimes involved with the craft, one such, being Joseph Hedley of Homer Lane, Warden, near Hexham, who became famous for his quilting and fine designs. As a young man Hedley was apprenticed to a tailor, but he did not care much for the work and appears to have left it to design and make quilts for both rich and poor, becoming known as 'Old Joe the Quilter' or 'Quilter Joe'. He married, and the couple lived in a small cottage in Homer Lane where they kept hens and had a small garden. When his wife became ill Hedley nursed her until her death about four years later, after which he carried on quilting despite ever-failing sight. In 1825, he was brutally murdered, supposedly for the money he made from quilting. The mystery of his murder was never solved. At the time of his death Mr A. Wright wrote a poem about him, from which these are a few verses:

Joe was beloved by all. The great
Forgit the lowness of his state,
And at their tables sometimes sate
    Respected Joe the Quilter.

By efforts of superior skill
He paid these tokens of good will;
Humble but independent still
    Was grateful Joe the Quilter.

His quilts with country fame were crown'd
So neatly stitch'd and all the ground
Adorn'd with flowers, or figured round,
   Oh clever Joe the Quilter.

Who raised the tale 'twere vain to scan,
But far and wide the story ran
That there was scarce a wealthier man
   Than poor old Joe the Quilter.

Quilts are not only nice to look at but are warm and practical. Not everyone in the Durham area had a hand-made Durham quilt, but for those who did it was a prized possession, something to be kept for best occasions. Families who had more than one quilt often had a good white one for best, and others, such as 'strippies', which were possibly not as well made or designed, for everyday use. This was con-

Fig. 2 *A very fine turkey red and white strip quilt with typical running feather pattern*

firmed by Mrs Graham of Southwick who, at the age of 74, told me how she had come by her quilt. Her mother had bought it from a Miss Nottingham for whom it had been made in a quilt club when she was to be married. She was jilted by her fiancé and, no longer wanting to keep it, she offered the quilt to Mrs Graham's mother for the sum of 30s, the price that she had paid, but was actually paid £2. The quilt was made in the 1890s and is blue with a border of flowers on a fawn ground. It had never been used. It was handed down to her daughter, who can only remember it being on the bed twice, once when she had her baby and another time when she was ill and the doctor was coming. The quilt has never been washed and is in good condition because it has always been kept wrapped up and stored in a suitcase. This is not unusual; a number of quilts are found in good condition as they, too, have been kept for special occasions and much prized.

Girls learned their skills from their mothers: Mrs Horan of Wingate, who is in her seventies, told me that she learned from her mother, as did her mother before her, and also her grandmother before that. It appeared that her family had always been quilters. Mrs Horan said that from the age of eight she helped her mother dress the quilt frame, threaded needles, and collected the money for the quilt club. She threaded 50 needles at a time – each had to have $3\frac{1}{2}$ yards of thread. The quilt frame must have been placed under the window for light as the little girl pinned the needles in the window curtains and looped the thread, just once, around the needle so that it did not trail on the floor. As she grew older, she was allowed to stitch on the quilt. She sat on a cracket (a wooden stool with two flat sides and a V-shape cut out of the middle of the bottom edges, for legs). She was allowed to put cushions on the cracket to lift her up to the correct height to work. Mrs Elizabeth Wray, a quilter at South Hylton, had three sons, the youngest of whom remembers that he had to thread 50 needles before going out to play. There was strict discipline in these households and duties were carried out before any recreation.

The houses were very small and the quilt frame took up most of the space in a room. I have seen a large quilt frame in use, in a house in Weardale. It was in the 'front' room where the staircase led to the two rooms on the first floor. The frame was under the window and stretched all the way across the room, so that to get to the stairs, the quilt frame had to be lifted.

Quilt clubs were often run by miners' wives to help supplement the family income, as wages were very low. Mrs Horan remembers that her husband, who had a good job down the mine in the 1920s, came home with only 28s for a six-day working week in the Wingate pit. When he was married in 1908, her father had earned only 12–14s a week, but was only paid once a fortnight. Mr Arthur Marley remembers his father getting 6s 6d a shift, working six days a week (39s a week) at Monkwearmouth colliery, before the General Strike in 1926, but when he went back after 26 weeks, they were paid only 30s a week. Mr Marley told me that railwaymen at that time

earned £2 a week and were considered well off compared to the miners. Miss Flintoff, a teacher, vividly remembers her first pay packet in 1919, it was £10 6s 8d a month (£2 7s 8½d a week). The suffragette movement had only just managed to get the vote for women in the previous year, and male teachers would have received a higher salary. In an office, Miss Flintoff's sister earned 17s 6d a week, and a female shop assistant in the same period would earn 15s a week.

To put wages and the price of quilts in perspective there are a number of considerations to be made. The prices of food in shops varied then as much as today, and much depended upon quality, the manufacture and where you made your purchase. Here are approximate costs of some everyday foodstuffs in the 1920s: potatoes at 2s a stone (14lb = 1 stone) were expensive; bread was 2½d a small loaf; granulated sugar 3d pound, or 3s 8d stone; plain flour 2s 4d–2s 10d a stone; yeast 1d–1½d for 2oz; loose tea 2s–3s 8d per lb. Out of the small wage packet the weekly deductions such as rent, which in Mrs Graham's case was 14s 6d a week, burial insurance and possibly clothing or boot club money had to come first, then most of what was left went on food. If, after the weekly deductions were made, there was not much left for food, the family went hungry. About half the food money was spent on bread, which was the staple diet. Life was not easy for the poorly paid, such as the miners.

The price of a quilt in the 1920s was about 30s but varied according to the quilter running the club and the amount of work put into the quilt – extras, such as a star centre, had to be paid for. The instalment plan was used, people paid the standard weekly charge of one shilling. Despite the poverty, there seemed to be no lack of people wanting to join a club.

There appears to have been great community spirit, and, even though there was great hardship, everyone pulled together. People living in the same area all worked at the same place, so all knew one another. Their houses were rented from the 'bosses', who built rows of small terraced cottages. In a town, therefore, there were separate community areas where railway men, miners, shipyard workers, or professional people would live. Small wonder that friends and relatives lived in close proximity to each other. The same was true of the villages; often almost the whole village would work at one pit, so if tragedy struck, the whole village suffered.

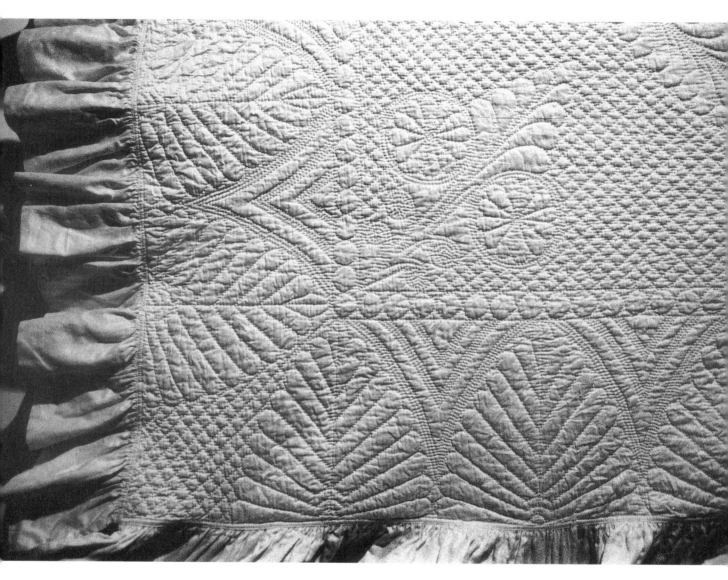

Fig. 3 *Corner of cream sateen quilt with leaf motif and very interesting infill, making use of close rows of stitching for a good definition*

The small lead-mining village of Rookhope in Weardale is a typical example of a closely-knit community. Mr Thomas Emmerson Heatherington, now 80, tells how the men were so poorly paid – in the 1900s around 28s a week – that they would try to get secondary work, jobbing on farms. His father did drystone walling and pig-sticking for extra money. Each house had a garden, so no one ever bought vegetables. Depending upon the size of the garden, you had a chicken and a pig; if large (not a field), you had a cow, pig and chicken. Coal was brought in by the wagon load, each load costing £5.

This helpfulness and community spirit was also strong among the women, who worked in their homes from morn till dusk, for it was considered a sin for a woman to be idle. They usually had large families to look after. In the case of Mrs Heatherington, there were six children, his mother and an ageing aunt as well as herself and her husband. The men started work at 6 am and had to leave home by 5.15 as they had to walk three miles to get to the mine. The women worked a long day, as they had to get up and see to their husbands' breakfast and get their lunch ready, after which they blackleaded the range, made breakfast for the rest of the family, fed any animals, baked, washed, and so on. Only in the evening was there time to quilt. Sunday was an exception, as the women only made the midday meal, as the ashes

Fig. 4 *Pink sateen quilt in St Barnabas pattern with, centre rose. The 'wineglass' pattern is used as an infill. Made by Christ Church Quilt Group*

had been taken out of the fire on the Saturday night. They attended chapel three times in the day, and only the Bible and two magazines, *The Joyful News* and the *Sunday Companion*, were allowed to be read.

Quilting was mainly a winter occupation, using the dim light of oil lamps and candles. Whenever anyone needed a quilt all the neighbours and friends gathered to help. It was possibly the only time that they had for relaxation and gossip. The women would don long white 'gauntlets' to cover their arms from the wrist to above the elbow; this was to keep the quilt clean and free from snags. (Washing was no easy task in those days.) It usually took a week to make a quilt and during that time no housework was done. If no one was in need of a quilt, they used to 'put one in' and work it for

the Chapel Bazaar, to raise money.

When the miners' wives ran a quilt club, the number of members varied between 20 and 50 according to the person running it. The length of time needed to produce a quilt varied from club to club, but quite often it took only one week. Perhaps others did as Mrs Horan, and worked until 2 or 3 o'clock in the morning, still getting up next morning to see their husbands off to work and make sandwiches for their meal. Mrs Horan said that she could work better at night as there were no interruptions, one of the problems of the home worker. Sometimes a quilter would work alone, so as to keep all the stitches alike, but sometimes she had help from

Fig. 5 *Corner of St Barnabas pattern worked by members of Christ Church Quilt Group*

the family, sisters, aunts and children.

Mrs Marley had 50 people in her club, paying 1s a week, and it took four to five days to complete a quilt. Her youngest son, Mr Arthur Marley, is now about 70 years of age, and clearly remembers when he was very small seeing at least four and sometimes five people at the quilt frame in the kitchen. His four sisters and even his brother (a miner) learned to ply a needle, and became very proficient. Mrs Horan and her sister helped their mother. She in turn had help from her daughters and turned out one quilt a week. There were always 25 people in her club who paid 1s a week for 30 weeks. Another club took 20 people, who paid for one year. The number of members and the length of time to pay varied from club to club, but what did not seem to vary was the willingness of people to join and the desire to own a quilt.

Friday, it seems, was a day when most people left the quilt frame, as it was 'housekeeping day'. It was the day for scrubbing the table and outside steps, and doing the washing, though they tried to keep out of water as much as possible as it softened the hands. Soft hands were something that a quilter did not want, as the needle could then pierce the fingers more easily. Mrs Horan told me that her fingers often became black with bruising. The chalk used to mark the patterns would infect any sores. She would then put on a cabbage leaf to draw out any infection, after which bacon fat was put on to harden the skin. Some people used toilet soap

"The Comfy"
THE ORIGINAL
Size 80×95 Style

"The Comfy"

instead of bacon fat.

Saturday was usually the day for shopping and buying materials for the next quilt, and Sunday for marking and preparing the frame. The quilters tried to plan the work for the club so that every so often they had a week free, so that if needed they could catch up, or make something else, perhaps a special quilt.

Churches often had a sewing or quilting group, which worked on similar lines to the other quilt clubs, but with the money usually going towards something that was needed in the Church, or to a charity. One such group was organised at St Barnabas, Grangetown, Sunderland. This was started before the Second World War by Mrs Petrie, the vicar's wife. There were eight quilters, and another group making clippie mats, meeting in the same room. They originally

Fig. 6 *Factory-made machine quilt in plain green and patterned sateen with sawtooth lines sew lengthways –* circa *1920*

met once a week, but this soon became twice, Mondays and Wednesdays, as they enjoyed the afternoons so much. They each contributed food and had a lovely tea when they had finished working. Husbands were cajoled into helping them by making templates and doing any other such jobs. This church joined with Christ Church and the group was continued by Mrs Pickering, but after the move it slowly dwindled to four members. Because of the age of the members, the group finished in about 1975.

The pattern made by this group was always very similar, and so it was christened the 'St

Fig. 7 *Red, fawn and white North Country patchwork quilt, with wineglass pattern in the red borders, roses at the junctions and general infill of square diamonds*

Barnabas pattern', the rose and the fan being the main templates, cut out of plywood. Outlining was used, and the filling pattern was the wineglass. Mrs Pickering told me that she had to keep a strict eye upon the quality of the stitching, and would make a member unpick if it was not up to standard. Such a quilt was bought by Miss Flintoff for £17 in about 1950. Miss Flintoff had to buy her own material, which had to be from Binns' store in Sunderland, as they had a good stock and colour range of 'Silver sheen sateen'. This I am told was strong, of good quality and, most important of all, did not fade when in constant use. This cannot be said of all quilts, as some are so faded that one cannot tell the original colour, and others have only kept their colour because they have been kept out of the light. Another Church group was run by Mrs Esther Chambers at St Aidans, and again the quality of the work was strictly monitored, being pulled out at night if not up to standard.

There are some factory-made wadded quilts that bear a resemblance to the hand-made ones. One such is the 'Comfy' quilt, which was usually of a plain and a patterned sateen, completely reversible, with a large diamond in the middle. The quilting was done by machine and was in a zig-zag all-over pattern. These quilts seem to have been made between 1916 and 1925 and were possibly cheaper than those made by hand. Here are one or two advertisements from the *Sunderland Daily Echo*:

12 Jan 1916. "Comfy" quilted quilt. Extra double bed size. Sale price 17s 11d each. Worth 25s 6d – Blackets

31 January 1921. Bargain No. 511. 150 "Comfy" quilted quilts in various colourings, will wash well and never go lumpy. Size 70" × 90". Sale price 37s 6d each – Binns

18 February 1921. Amazing offer of "Comfy" quilted quilts. Size 1¾ × 2 yds. All bordered in pretty plain and figured sateens, some with diamond centre, in crimson, green, saxe and sky. Ordinary prices 39s 6d and 42s 6d. While they last, 25s each. We advise coming tomorrow for these – Blackets

From some of the quilts that I have seen, the claim made by Binns would appear to be correct, as they were not lumpy, though they were certainly well washed. Machine quilting produces a continuous line which lacks the lively intricate play of light and shade created by the regular, finely-spaced rhythm of hand quilting.

An organisation which helped to promote Durham Quilting and encouraged a high standard of craftsmanship was the Women's Institute in Co. Durham. Under the guidance of Mrs Alice Armes, the handicrafts organiser for DFWI, the institute stimulated interest and demand for quilting in the 1920s, insisting upon a high standard of technique and design. Through her efforts, traditional quilting was included in schedules in WI handicraft exhibitions in Durham and also at the National Federation, and Durham quilting began to be known amongst handicraft people throughout the country.

Quilts from the area are not always entirely of one colour; some are multicoloured, with a patchwork top being used. But in the Durham area, the quilting itself is considered to be of prime importance, and in the most beautiful examples the plain-coloured material shows off best the subtlety of the technique.

2
QUILTS

Quilts are now collectors' items, and can sometimes be found in antique shops and at auction sales. Their condition varies, and some still have the original blue marking lines drawn by the 'stamper', the person who marked the pattern. These blue lines were usually drawn by professional markers, for which the quilt was sent away, or by an itinerant quilter, and could be erased by two or three washings. Quilts in this condition show that they were treasured and rarely used, and consequently fetch a higher price when sold.

Some of the best places to see quilts are museums. The Bowes Museum in Barnard Castle usually has a number on display around the various rooms, and has others in store which can be seen by special appointment. The Shipley Art Gallery in Gateshead has a few, and the Beamish Museum has about 180, but unfortunately these cannot be seen, as they are kept in storage. Maybe one day they will be available for study, even if not for the general public to see. I am told they are of varying quality and the museum does have a catalogue with brief notes about them, which they are very willing to let you browse through.

Before 1900 white or ivory quilts were generally made and kept for best, with the 'strippy' being for everyday use. Some coloured quilts were made, but it was not until the 1890s and 1900s that coloured sateen material became popular.

The Strip Quilt was popular in northern England from the eighteenth century onwards. Strips of printed cotton or plain material were sewn together lengthways. They were often 7–9 inches wide, but I have seen a quilt with four white strips of 14 inches and the other, red, ones

of $9\frac{1}{2}$ inches. Another blue and white quilt had large stripes down the centre with narrowing ones towards the outside.

Strips usually alternated a colour with white. Turkey red, pink or blue were popular, the latter two sometimes being seen together. (See Fig. 2.) Many have a white backing material.

Quite often strip quilts are quilted with four different border patterns, each running down the entire length and generally just the width of the stripe. Patterns do not necessarily follow in sequence, but usually the two outside strips are the same. One such sequence is as follows:

Pattern one, 1, 8, 12 strips; pattern two, 2, 5, 9 strips;
pattern three, 3, 6, 11 strips; pattern four, 4, 7, 10 strips

The domestic sewing machine became widely available around the middle of the nineteenth century. Now, with the help of a machine, strips could be put together much faster.

Strip patterns are sometimes used instead of a central motif, either with or without a border, on quilts of one colour. A popular border, on an otherwise plain quilt, was a cream floral print sateen. One of these quilts was made in Grangetown, Sunderland, in 1912 for Ellen Maud Summerville on her marriage. (See colour plate) This is designed with a 13-inch border and a blue centre, which unfortunately is fugitive. Both these and the backing material are of sateen. The reverse is blue with a very strong stylised pattern of flowers. Often the backing material bears no resemblance to the front, possibly as this was not meant to be seen. A similar quilt was made for the marriage of Miss Nottingham, *c.* 1890. It has a very similar cream

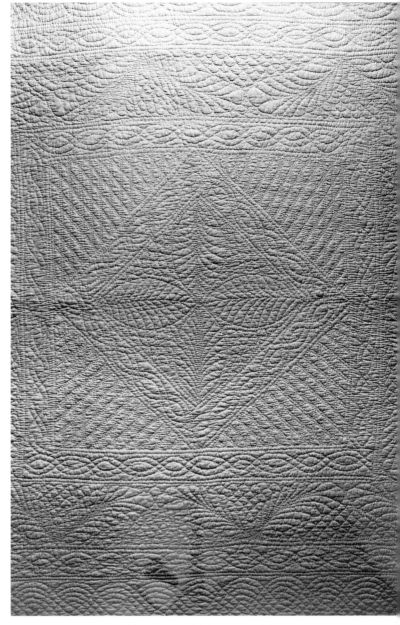

Fig. 8 *Central motif of a white quilt; note the good definition given by close lines of stitchery*
Fig. 9 *Feathers, leaves, trail and pincushion are patterns used on this white quilt,* circa *1890. Note unusual use of lines making the filling pattern around the central motif*

floral print border and blue centre, but the reverse is in a bright gold.

Around the beginning of the eighteenth century, patchwork, sometimes called pieced work, became a fashionable way of using up scraps of material. From the beginning of the nineteenth century printed cottons replaced silks, satins and furnishing fabrics as popular materials. Patchwork also became an acceptable genteel occupation, so poor and well-off alike, though for different reasons, sewed scraps of material left over from dresses into various patterns. Those in poor circumstances sometimes used the better part of a worn out garment to cut into

patches to make a quilt. As my old Granny said many times, 'waste not, want not'.

Coloured patchwork was a set-back to quilters, as their art could best be seen on plain material, not printed cottons. However, they adapted their designs and became inventive in making the old techniques fit into new shapes. A popular beginners' patchwork pattern was known as 'Grandmother's Flower Garden'. This used hexagons which were put together in rosettes, after which they could be sewn in various combinations, sometimes with a plain fabric dividing the 'flowers'. The six 'petals' of a rosette were usually made from the same colour

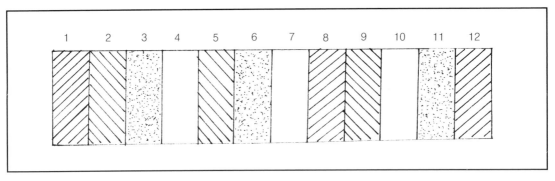

Fig. 10 *Chart showing the order of the four patterns used on a strip quilt,* circa *1880*

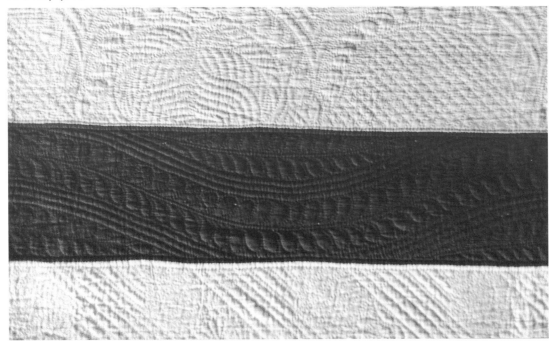

Fig. 11 *Unusual border pattern on just one white strip of this quilt*

or patterned fabric, but the centre could be different – plain, as opposed to a pattern, or possibly a large flower.

With the old utilitarian quilts, centralising a flower appears not to have been of prime importance, perhaps because of the lack of extra material, or because it was wasteful, or more likely both. However, there was often ingenuity and skill shown in the blending of colours, clever use of small patterned prints or stripes and cutting out of different repeat patterns to obtain subtle variations. These have a charm all of their own.

Other patterns found frequently are the Flower Basket, which is made with triangles and an applied handle; the Jockey Cap; the Pincushion (Peter and Paul); the Windmill and the Star. Colour plate 1, a very striking red and white quilt, uses a small-patterned material and plain white, and employs the Dog Tooth pattern to make the four borders used to separate the coloured areas.

Quilting patterns used on patchwork quilts depend upon the design made by the pieces of material, and often follow the outline with infills where necessary. Various diamond filling patterns are popular as flowers. A pink-and-white flower basket quilt belonging to Mrs Sue Fielding is an example of this. The basket is outlined, while the rest of the square is quilted with a $\frac{1}{2}$-inch square diamond filling pattern. The alternating plain white squares have a 24-petalled round flower with leaves as a filling. There is also an interesting border using this flower in an oval

Fig. 12 *Strip patterns on blue and white star quilt*

shape. Today, many lively patterns are made using both geometric shapes and scenes such as landscapes or children's nursery rhymes.

There are different methods of sewing patches together. Both use templates to cut out the fabric, but not for the American method there is just one template or paper pattern to draw or cut round, whereas the English template for one shape consists of either two metal ones, one being a cut-out of the other, or one metal and one plastic which is larger by the turning margin. The smaller of the two templates is to draw round on thickish paper or thin card – in the past people used to use old envelopes or letters. The second, larger template is for use on the material. The 'hole', or see-through plastic is there first to centralise the template on the pattern, or keep on the straight of the grain, and second, as it is made with a seam allowance, it can be drawn round, giving even turnings on all patches.

The American method of working is much quicker than the English. No paper templates

Fig. 13 *Grandmother's flower garden quilt by Ann Hayes, made over many years from remains of dress materials*

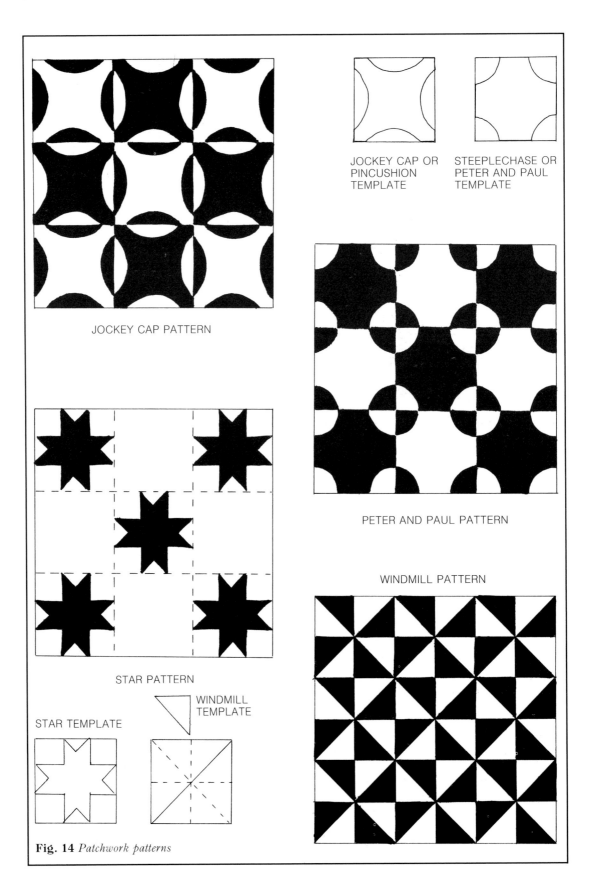

JOCKEY CAP OR PINCUSHION TEMPLATE

STEEPLECHASE OR PETER AND PAUL TEMPLATE

JOCKEY CAP PATTERN

PETER AND PAUL PATTERN

WINDMILL PATTERN

STAR PATTERN

WINDMILL TEMPLATE

STAR TEMPLATE

Fig. 14 *Patchwork patterns*

are used. The patches are put right sides together and sewn with a running stitch or machine stitch. Great accuracy needs to be taken when cutting the material and in the sewing to make sure that all seam allowances are equal, otherwise when the patch is completed it will not lie flat. It is advisable to check the templates at the outset, fitting them together like a jigsaw puzzle, to see if there are any gaps, thus necessitating adjustments. Templates very easily become inaccurate with constant use.

The English method of working is to fold the material over the paper template and tack. When sufficient of these are ready, two are placed with the right sides back to back and then oversewn together with very tiny close stitches. Repeat until the whole pattern has been built.

A new large Durham quilt has been designed and made by Mrs Evelyn Fox of Sunderland, using traditional templates left to her by her grandmother Mrs Elizabeth Wray, who ran a quilt club before the First World War. The quilt, which uses a three plait and feathers among its patterns, is cream cotton on one side and patterned apricot cotton on the other, with a filling of 2oz weight polyester wadding.

Traditional methods do not necessarily mean

Fig. 15 *Quilted and patchwork motifs from a pink and white quilt,* circa *1900. There are 36 alternating 11-inch squares of pink and white basket patchwork and plain white squares, divided by one-inch strips of pink. The 10-inch border is made of a band of pink and a band of white. The whole surface is closely quilted*

traditional patterns. Some quilts made today are pictorial. One such quilt, designed and made by Mrs Sue Fielding, uses the countryside for inspiration with a central panel of poppies, fields, hills and clouds. The deep border has clusters of trees with small animals among them, such as a rabbit, squirrel, bird, butterfly, and even a cat. The leaves are represented by applied shapes quilted separately on the sewing machine. The material is fawn curtain-lining on the top side and brown poly-cotton on the reverse, with 4oz polyester wadding in the middle.

Many people have old quilts that are well washed and worn so that sometimes the pattern is very difficult to read. One reason could be that there is not enough definition between the pattern and the background. At times these quilts appear to be used for purposes other than bed coverings, as I have seen one in use as a car cover in cold weather, another by a car me-

Fig. 16 *The first quilt made by Evelyn Fox using some of her grandmother's templates*

chanic to lie on the floor, another as a dust sheet for a painter. Even in today's technological age they have their utilitarian uses.

Designing a Quilt

When starting one needs to decide upon the size, whether for a double bed, single bed or cot. From there, patterns are played around with until a design forms in the mind and on paper. Considerations mentioned in the following chapters must be taken into account, and when the enjoyment of making patterns is near completion, accurate drawings must be made.

Folding paper is a good way to get the necessary accurate divisions. First fold in half, then in half again, then open out. Fold each of these quarters in half, accurately, then open out your paper, revealing an eight-point star. If desired, a ruler and pencil can be used to mark these divisions more clearly. If more divisions are needed for guidance, just fold the paper again.

An accurate drawing is now needed, for two reasons: one is to practise making the patterns; the second is a final check to see if proportion, balance and definition are correct. Use a piece of paper one quarter of the size of the quilt if designing in the traditional way with templates, and mark out accurately. If an asymmetrical design is being created, then perhaps a larger sheet of paper is needed to draw out the whole design.

Draw in your chosen filling pattern, then stand back and look critically at the overall design. Does the main pattern stand out? Would it look better with more definition, and, if so, how? Would a smaller background make it look more dense, or does it need one, two or three close outlines?

Fig. 17 *Countryside quilt by Sue Fielding, 1983*

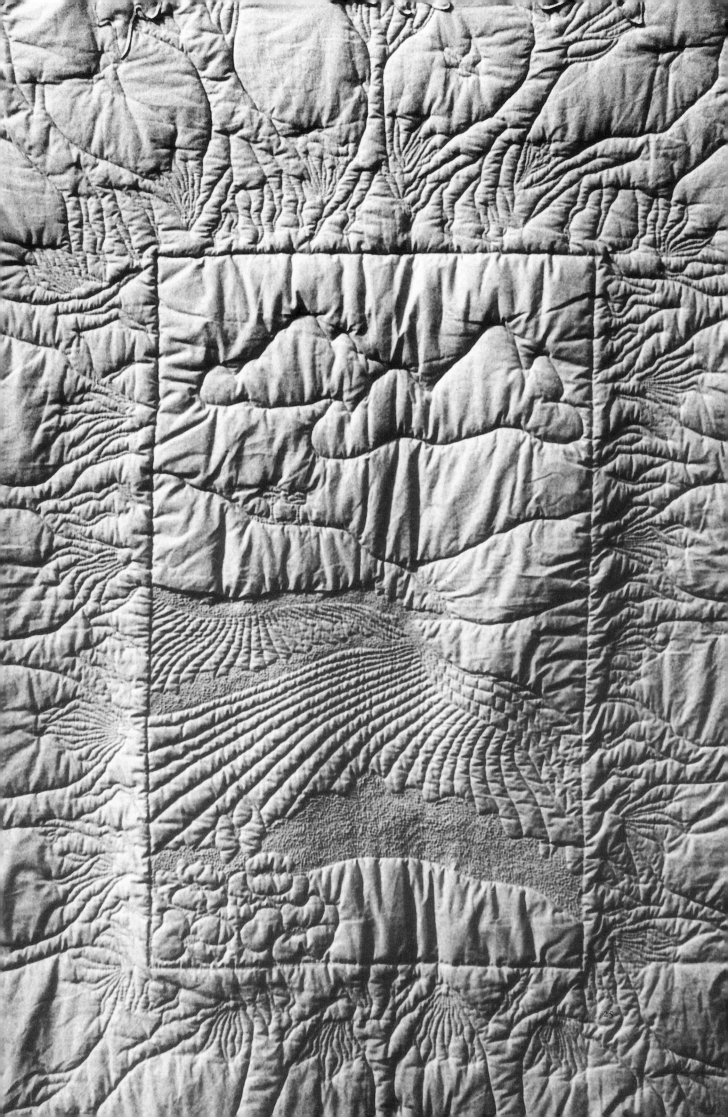

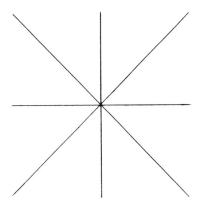

Fig. 18 *Eight-pointed star*

Having had drawing practice, prepare your materials, tack in your eight-pointed (or larger) star and any other guidelines necessary to keep your pattern accurate. Then mark your quilt top, dress the frame and quilt. Further help on individual points is given in the following chapters.

3
TEMPLATES OLD AND NEW

A template is a shape which has been cut out of card or another material. A stencil is the shape left after the template has been cut out (providing that it has been cut out in one piece).

Many traditional templates, as you would expect, take their patterns from nature, e.g. goosewing, goosetail, feather, rose, leaf, clam shell, and wave. Templates taken from man-made objects include the plait, hammock and chain. The chain could have been taken from the strong metal chains used in heavy industry, or similarly from the daisy chains we all used to make as children. Then there is the Weardale Wheel, which I suspect developed after the Kilhope water-wheel was built in upper Weardale in about 1860. This stands an impressive 40 feet high and was used to power the crushing machinery of the lead-mining firm of Park Level Mill. In about 1890 the mill went out of use, and the wheel is now conserved by Durham County Council.

Templates can be made out of virtually anything, and in the past card from boxes was used by miners' wives, for example, as it was easily come by, and could be replaced when damaged. Sometimes wives would get their husbands to make templates for them: for example, Mrs Pickering's husband cut them out of plywood. Others were made out of metal and sometimes riveted together in the centre so that they would open out like a flower, like Mrs Hayes' grandmother's.

Accuracy in drawing round a template is essential. When making the outline, keep the pencil vertical so that the line is equidistant from the template all the way round. To show how inaccurate templates can become through lack of concentration, make a template of a circle, marking the edge in one place, then draw round it with the pencil sloping to the right, and cut out. Draw round this new template, placing the mark in the same spot as before. Re-draw, again with the pencil sloping to the right, and cut out. After repeating this a few times you will see that you no longer have a circle.

A symmetrical template can be checked for accuracy by simply drawing round, cutting out and folding into two or four as the case may be. A template tracing may be enlarged or reduced, as shown at the end of this chapter, by making a grid. This method is used when the size of a complicated design has to be changed.

The Feather is a typical Durham and North Country pattern. It is a very versatile one, and, if desired, can fill almost any shape. When drawing round a feather template, one has only the semi-circles on the outside for guidance, and so it is up to the individual worker to fill in the major part in her own way. This is how some of the variations evolve. A good feather has full, well-rounded shapes which curve down towards a middle spine. A bad feather has straight lines joining the outside to the middle.

Feathers can vary in many ways – they can be straight, curved, curled, large or small, continuous, fat or thin. The feathering can be joined down the central spine in one, two, or many lines. The latter tends to emphasise the pattern beautifully. Different shapes, e.g. triangles, squares or rectangles, can be filled by feathering. When made into a circle it is called a circlet, but when the circle is filled it is called a rose, as it resembles a flower. The main thing to remember when feathering is to make good, full, rounded shapes.

Fig. 19 *Off-white quilt with two broad borders divided by a narrow one. The running feather has a good central definition*

Fig. 20 *Rose, Wave Border, Clam Shell, Leaf, Goose Wing and Goose Tail*

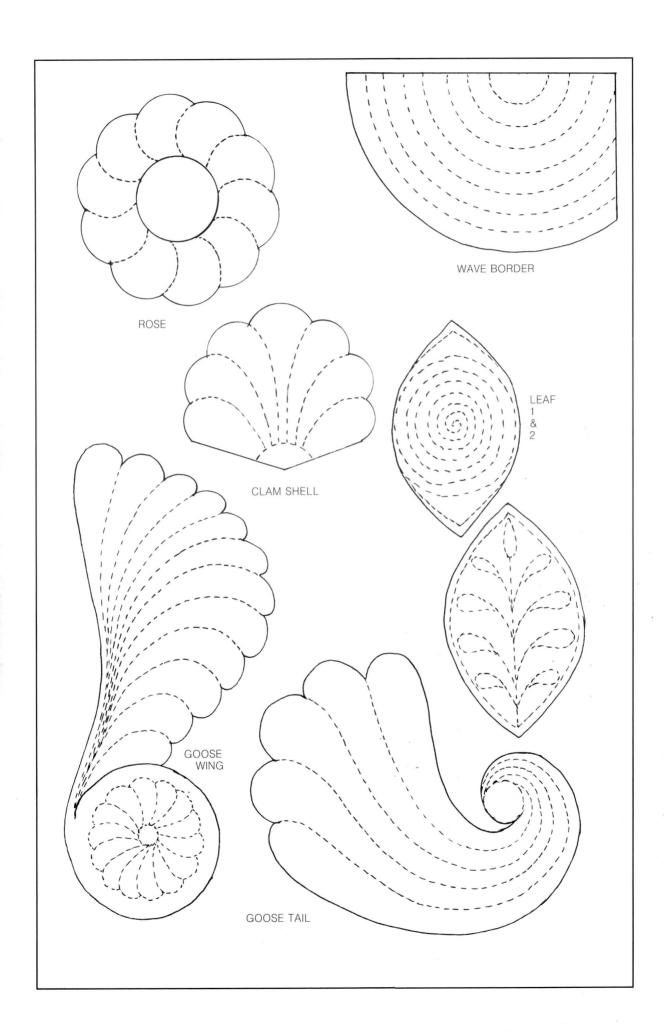

ROSE

WAVE BORDER

CLAM SHELL

LEAF
1
&
2

GOOSE
WING

GOOSE TAIL

Fig. 21 *Two metal folding templates made for Mrs Ann Butterfield of Trimdon,* circa *1900*

Fig. 22 *Feathers*

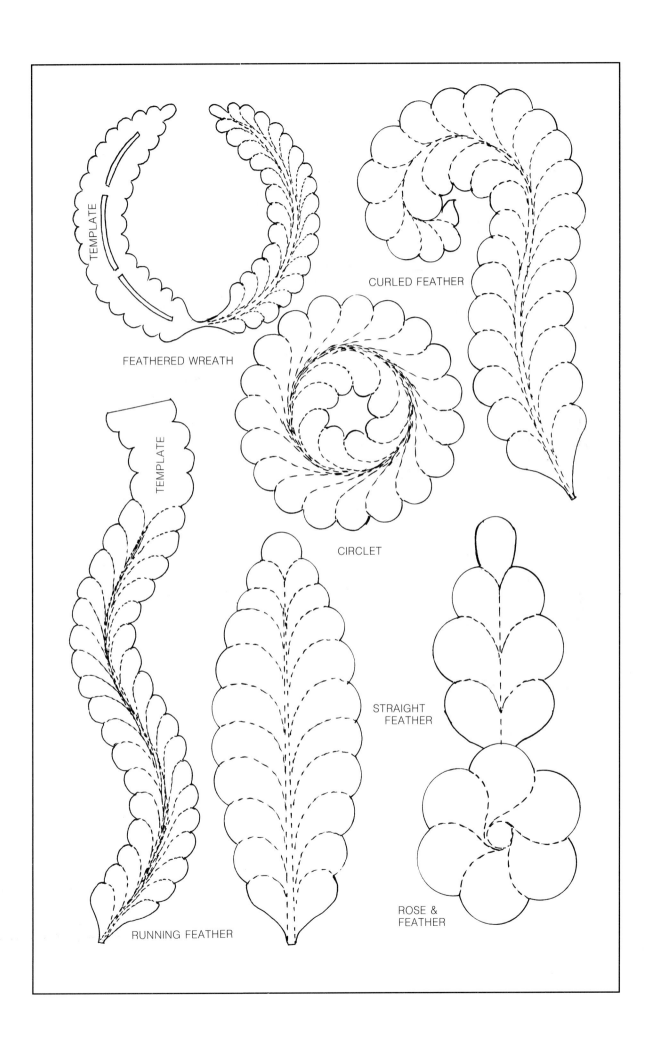

TEMPLATE

FEATHERED WREATH

CURLED FEATHER

TEMPLATE

CIRCLET

STRAIGHT
FEATHER

RUNNING FEATHER

ROSE &
FEATHER

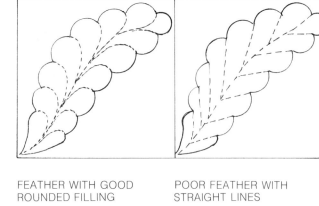

Fig. 23 *Running feather giving a 'bellows' all-over pattern on a large white cotton quilt*

FEATHER WITH GOOD
ROUNDED FILLING

POOR FEATHER WITH
STRAIGHT LINES

Fig. 24 *Good and bad feathers*

Fig. 25 *Feathered shapes*

1.
A North of England patchwork quilt, showing the striking use of two alternating colours. Interesting borders have been created using the saw-tooth or dog-tooth pattern.

2.
Close-up of above showing an interesting filling pattern in the white triangle, and a twist pattern in the saw-tooth border. The central motif has a floral design.

3.
Durham strip quilt circa *1880*
using four different running
designs.

4.
Close-up of Durham strip quilt
showing three of the different
patterns.

BORDER PLAIT

FAN

LINED HAMMOCK

FEATHERED HAMMOCK

HEART

WEARDALE WHEEL

Fig. 26 *Border plait, Fan, Lined hammock, Feathered hammock, Heart, Weardale wheel*

The True Lovers' Knot. This is sometimes used in the Durham area and at first sight looks to be a complicated pattern. It is a continuous ribbon-like line that weaves its way under and over. There are two ways of doing the Lovers' Knot, which look quite different from one another yet are similar, having only a slight variance in the template. This is just the angle of a curved line. The weaving on both follows the same pattern.

A simple way of constructing a template for the first knot is by taking one-eighth of a circle and marking one side into eight equal parts, numbering from the fat part of the wedge to the centre, the point being no. 9. Draw a curved line from 2 to 8, then a wide oval curve from 1 to 6. Make it into a double line by joining 2 to 5, and make the long line the same width by joining 9 to the second to top line, as in the diagram. The knot is constructed by drawing round the template each time in an eighth of a circle; first one way, then reversing it.

The template for the second knot can be made the same way, but with the wide oval line starting at 3 instead of 1. Alternatively, it can be constructed with a symmetrical tear shape. Draw round the tear twice, overlap in the centre, then complete the elliptical shape. This is to be done in one quarter of a circle and is the equivalent of two drawings of the other template placed back-to-back. The Shipley Art Gallery, Gateshead, has a template like this belonging to Mrs Hope of Chester-le-Street. I find that this template gives a smoother, continuous, ribbon-like flow. Both styles of lovers' knot are found on quilts.

Having now got the outline, from either of the templates, the connecting lines must be drawn to obtain a knot. With your hand going clockwise and starting from the centre, make the ribbon go over at A, under at B and over at C, then under at A over B under C and over at D. Repeat this on all four segments, and you should have a True Lovers' Knot.

The Twist. This is a very versatile template, as it can have different fillings, which give rise to different names. It can also be drawn around in different ways. Like the plait it can be fat or thin and it is nice to try out your pattern with both to see which is the most effective, though usually it is the fatter one.

To make the template, draw a circle, mark the middle and draw a horizontal line through (see Fig. 28). Extend the circle at the sides towards

the line, making an eye shape. Put a small similar shape in the centre. All that is missing are the two notches which help the correct positioning of the template when making patterns. These are placed diagonally opposite one another at an angle of between 25–45 degrees, from the central line, depending upon how large the hole is in the middle. A simple way to put the notches in the right place is to draw round your eye-shaped template, including the hole. Remove the template and replace it with the point C just touching the right inner point on the central hole, marked H, then draw around again. The top notch can be marked where the top line of the second shape touches the first line on the right side, and the bottom notch where the second shape touches the bottom line on the left. Cut out the notches and your template is complete.

Another way to make the eye-shaped template is to take a piece of paper and fold it into four. In the folded corner cut out a small rounded shape, then repeat this shape nearer the open edge, so that when the paper is opened it reveals this eye or leaf shape. This method was demonstrated to me by Mrs Horan when she showed me some of the patterns she used while running her quilt club.

The simple twist is constructed by drawing around the template from A to point B and around the hole, then notch C to point D. Move the template, putting point A to point H with the top notch touching the line of last twist. Repeat the drawing for as many times as required. It is a good idea to have a straight guide line in order that your border does not get an unwanted bend.

Other types of twist can be made and are found in old quilts, the *Lined Twist* being very popular. This is drawn the same way as the simple one, but is filled with extra lines. When used in strip patterns and borders the twist can be 9 inches or more in width and filled with at least 7 lines. The *Feathered Twist* and *Half-Feathered Twist* are reasonably common, and there are many other variations besides.

By using this same template, but without the notches, another set of variations can be made, such as the *Weardale Chain*. To achieve this, draw around the outside of the template once; draw a temporary line from point A through point D, which will later be removed; place point A on the centre of the pattern and re-draw, continuing as desired. This has a simple rose of four or more petals in the diamond shape made

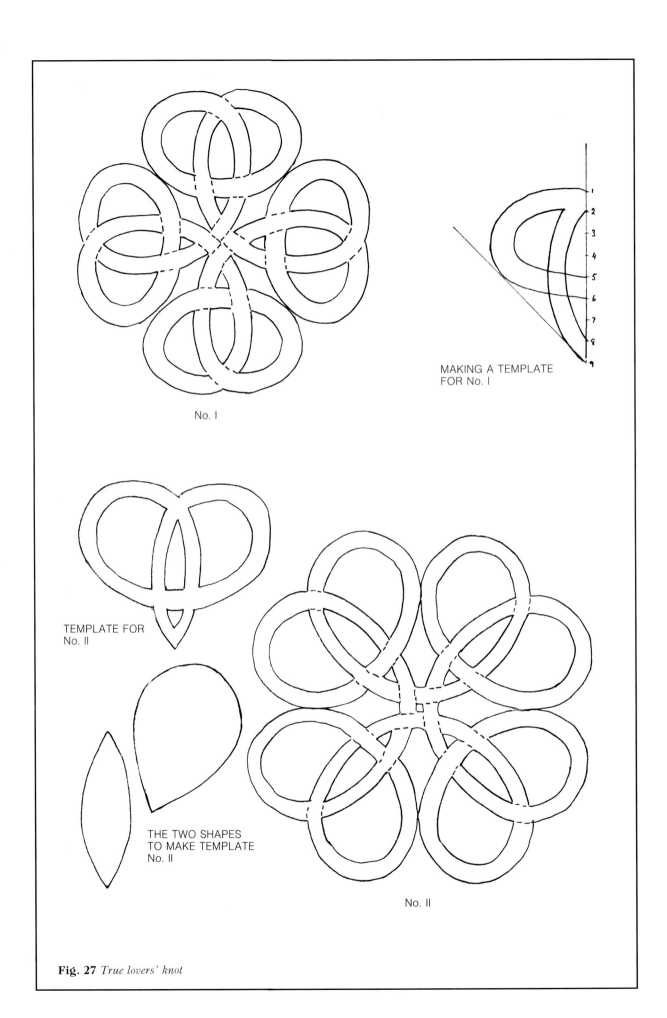

MAKING A TEMPLATE
FOR No. I

No. I

TEMPLATE FOR
No. II

THE TWO SHAPES
TO MAKE TEMPLATE
No. II

No. II

Fig. 27 *True lovers' knot*

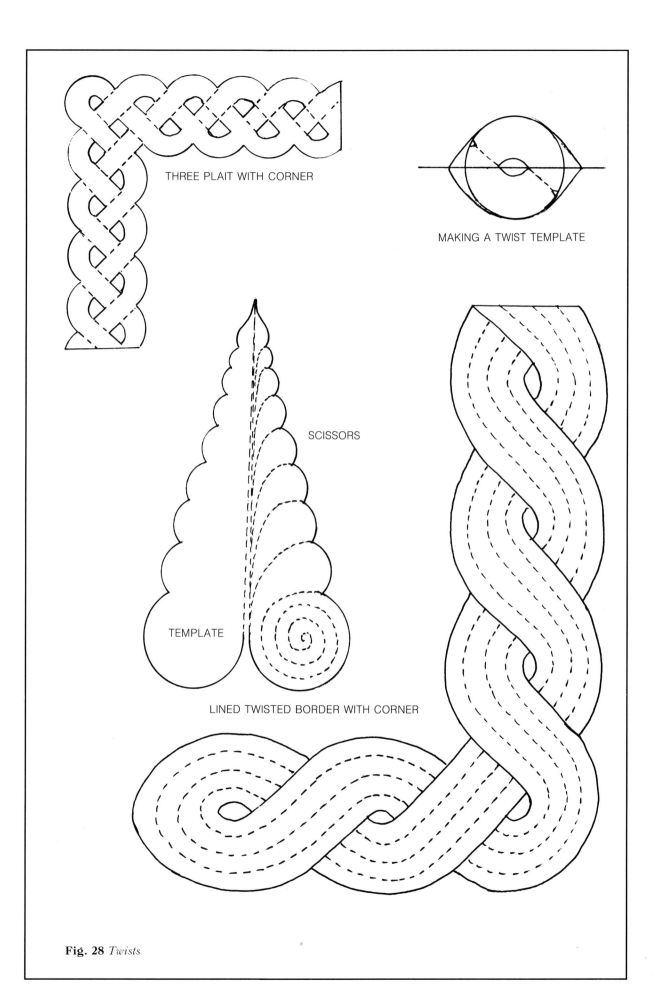

THREE PLAIT WITH CORNER

MAKING A TWIST TEMPLATE

SCISSORS

TEMPLATE

LINED TWISTED BORDER WITH CORNER

Fig. 28 *Twists*

WEARDALE CHAIN

TRAIL

PINCUSHION

LINED AND FEATHERED
TWIST

Fig. 29 *Patterns using twist template*

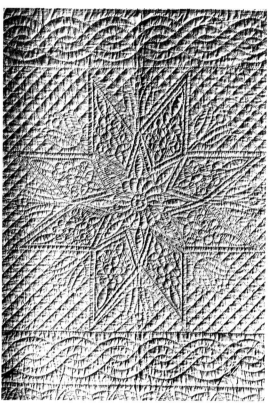

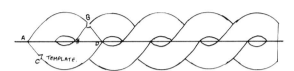

Fig. 30 *A simple twist*

Fig. 31 *Centre of 'Star Quilt' showing quilting patterns adapted to patchwork design*

Fig. 32 *Green sateen quilt by Mrs Elizabeth Wray,* circa *1900, with large pincushion (twist variation) border and smaller twist border, outlined with three rows of stitching for definition*

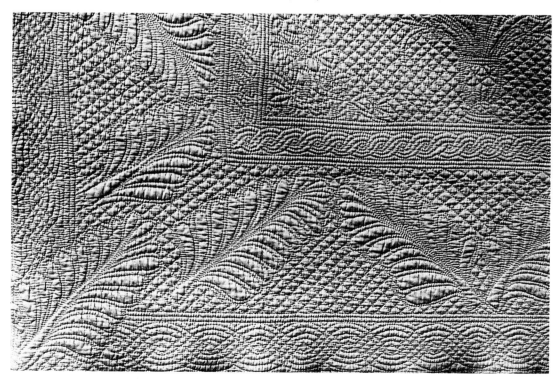

by the overlap, and the fan-type shape is filled in with lines which curve down to the point, making a very effective border.

The Plait. The most common plait in quilts is the three plait. It makes a lovely border pattern and is useful, as it is just a little thicker than the twist. As with the twist, a fatter, rounded template looks richer than a long thin one, but the most important thing with this template is that the ribbon-like lines must appear to follow through and flow well. It can of course be made in any size. Less common is the four plait, for which I have a template, but as yet have never seen on a quilt.

The Flat Iron. This is to be found many times and was one which Elizabeth Sanderson used a great deal. She had a distinctive method of filling in this shape, with characteristic leaves and scrolls. The template looks rather like a very large symmetrical leaf, but would, no doubt, have been made originally by placing two flat irons down on a piece of paper with their heels back-to-back so that the pointed ends were opposite and facing outwards. This outline could perhaps be made today using two electric irons, if they were not too long. This is quite a large shape which needs a pattern such as a rose, coil or feathering, or a combination, to fill the space.

The Hammock. This seems to be another design seen on old quilts. Unless drawn very small, it needs to have some filling. Most usual is a lined hammock, but it can also be linked, cabled or feathered. It can make a good border in combination with another template such as a fan, tassel, leaf or feather.

The Heart. This pattern is associated with marriage quilts, and there are many interpretations of this simple shape, either large or small, with or without fillings. It is sometimes used in border patterns and at other times to make a square or part of a larger motif.

The Fan. This seems to be a perennial favourite as it is so useful in combination with other templates to make up larger patterns or borders. It can be either a half fan or, more useful for corners, a quarter fan.

New templates can be made at any time. If you have a favourite shape that you know makes good patterns, why not make a template of it? Perhaps it is your favourite flower, which can be stylised or made free and maybe flowing.

Enlarging and reducing

There is a way of enlarging or reducing a pattern accurately for those less experienced at cutting or drawing templates for themselves – and for which you do not need to be a mathematician. You need a sheet of paper slightly larger than the proposed enlarged pattern, a ruler, a pencil and, preferably, a set square plus four narrow strips of paper which have one side perfectly straight (perhaps the edge of a magazine).

1. Draw round your template or make a copy of your tracing near the bottom left-hand corner of the sheet of paper and enclose this in a box.
2. Extend the top line A horizontally to the proposed length.
3. Extend the inside vertical line C for the required length to point D.
4. Make a diagonal line from the bottom left corner X through Y to the top of the page.
5. To complete the large box draw the last two lines – making sure that you have right-angled corners – until they touch the diagonal.
6. Now take a strip of paper and cut it accurately the length of line AY.
7. Fold this in two, then into quarters and again into eighths, but at each fold open it up so that there is only one thickness of paper. This makes for greater accuracy.
8. Hold this paper on the line AY and mark off the divisions.
9. Using the same strip, mark off on the opposite line XC.
10. Take another strip of paper and repeat for lines AX and YC.
11. Take a ruler and join all your marks so that you have a grid over your drawing.
12. The same procedure is followed as for marking the larger box.
13. If a complicated drawing is to be copied it is advisable (to make identification easier), to number and letter your grids.
14. All that remains to do is copy a line from the small grid into the corresponding grid in the large box. This can be done square by square, and when finished you should have an accurate copy.

Fig. 33 *Blue and cream crib quilt 21 inches by 15 inches, by author*

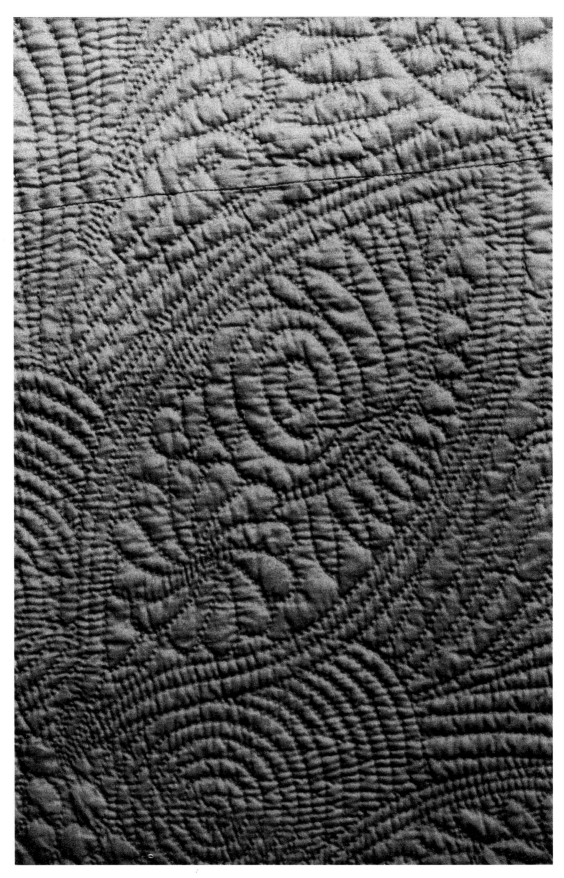

Fig. 34 *'Flat Iron' pattern on an Elizabeth Sanderson quilt in gold sateen*

Fig. 35 *Filling of a flat iron pattern worked in Rookhope by Mrs Elizabeth Heatherington,* circa *1900*

Fig. 36 *Double 'lined hammock' border pattern with 'leaves' and 'heart' on a quilt by Elizabeth Wray,* circa *1920*

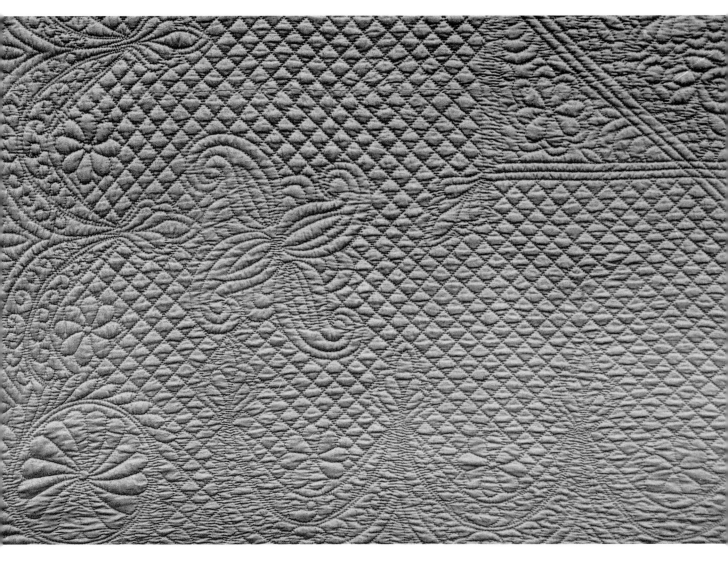

Fig. 37 *'Hammock' border with curl infill*

Fig. 38 *Corner motif on a Rookhope quilt, using hearts and arrows*
Heart border pattern from a blue and white 'Strippy'
Heart Motif made with folded paper similar to one belonging to Mrs Hope of Chester-le-Street (Now at the Shipley Art Gallery)

CORNER MOTIF ON A ROOKHOPE QUILT,
USING HEARTS AND ARROWS

HEART BORDER PATTERN
FROM A BLUE AND WHITE
'STRIPPY'

HEART MOTIF MADE WITH FOLDED
PAPER SIMILAR TO ONE BELONGING TO
MRS HOPE OF CHESTER-LE-STREET
(NOW AT THE SHIPLEY ART GALLERY)

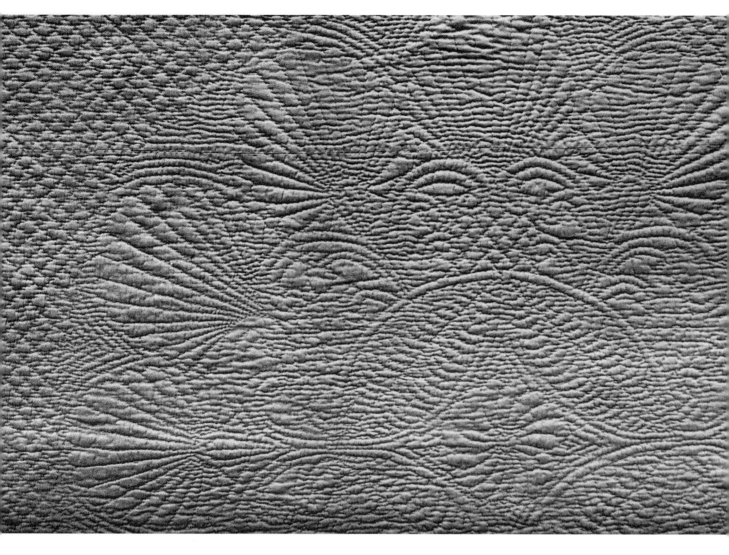

Fig. 39 *A 1912 deep pink sateen quilt with cream floral
border. Deep fan shapes complete the central motif*

Fig. 40 *Fan variations*

FAN VARIATIONS

A BORDER ON AN OFF-WHITE 'BEST' QUILT

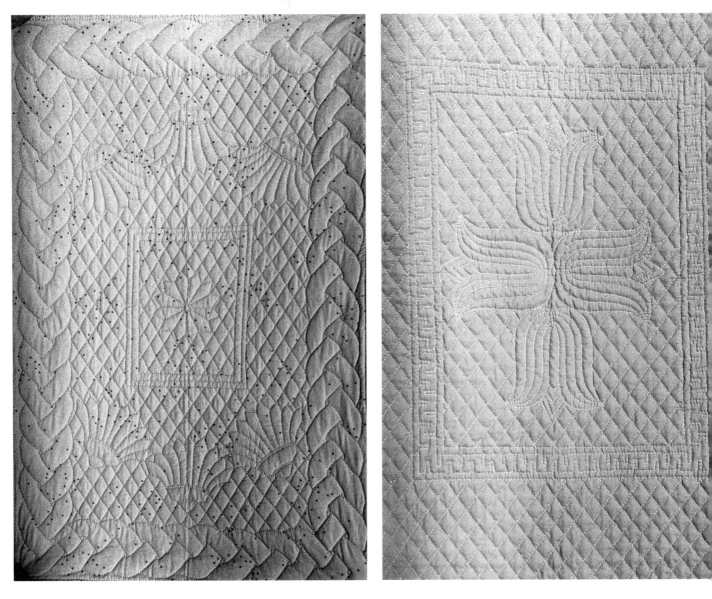

Fig. 41 *Cot quilt in pale blue material with dark blue stars which has a deep three-plait border. Designed by Gordon Hill and quilted by his wife Linda, 1987*

Fig. 42 *Small dark blue quilt, the first to be designed and made by Mr and Mrs Hill, 1987*

5.
Sateen quilt 94 inches × 80 inches in bright pink with the reverse in deep gold and alternate rows of running and curved feathers. The infill is a diamond pattern.

6.
Close-up of sateen quilt.

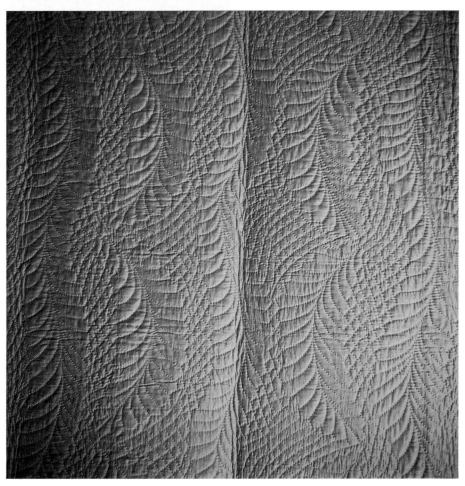

7.
Blue quilt with 13 inch floral border made in Grangetown, Sunderland in 1912. The overall size is 96 inches × 82 inches, is quilted from top to bottom with two alternating strip patterns starting with a twist on the outside, then a fan pattern which straddles both the floral border and the blue centre, finishing with a twist. The rows are divided by two lines half an inch apart.

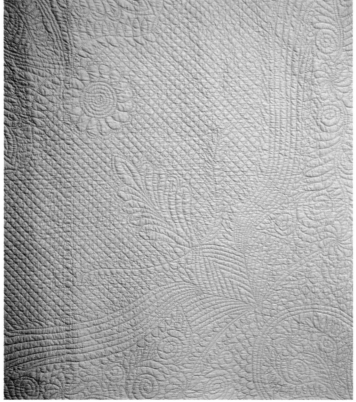

8.
Corner of an Allenheads designed quilt in typical Elizabeth Sanderson style. Gold with the reverse in fawn, size 95 inches × 86 inches with a large central motif and corner patterns meeting each other.

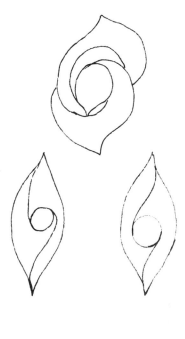

Fig. 43 *The centre of a wayside plant*

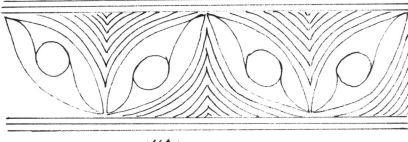

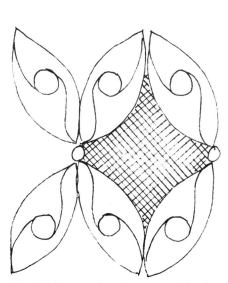

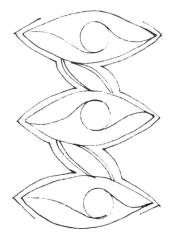

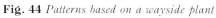

Fig. 44 *Patterns based on a wayside plant*

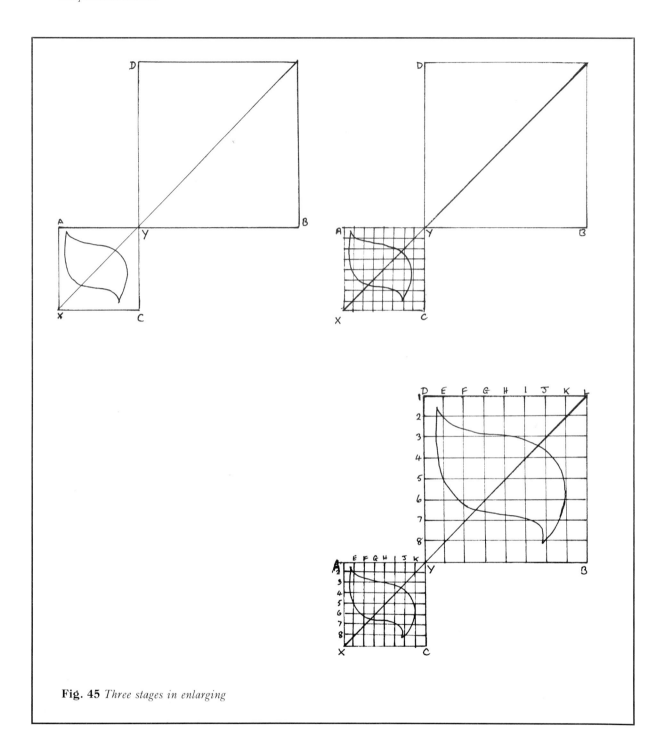

Fig. 45 *Three stages in enlarging*

4

PATTERNS AND INSPIRATION

Making patterns can be great fun. Just take a few templates and try them in different combinations. Do not get tense: relax. If the first few patterns do not look right, try again. Look at the idea as a child would and treat it as play; don't let the pressure of time inhibit you. With these few traditional templates, draw round them and see which 'sit' well together. Perhaps you are going to quilt a cushion cover to see if you like the method before starting on a large quilt. Take the templates which you like best and start putting them into various combinations. The patterns can be either symmetrical or asymmetrical, with borders around or not.

Look at some old quilts, and observe the economy in use of different templates (the usual number seems to be four). Notice how the central motif relates to the border, using the same patterns even if in different ways. When border patterns are used, note how they vary in size yet still use the same shapes, or use a small narrow border between various patterns, thus linking them together. The main thing about pattern-making is that all should blend well together to make a unified whole.

In the past, the majority of quilters drew their own patterns, but there were professional markers or 'stampers' – people who would mark out your quilt for a fee, which seemed to range from 1s to 1s 6d. Old Joe the quilter was one such person in the nineteenth century, and a little later the village of Allenheads became quite famous for the same thing; people would come from all over to have a quilt marked by George Gardener and, later, his apprentices. He kept the village shop and had a workroom at the back where he used to trim hats, then later drew patterns and marked quilts. He developed a

flowing personal style but was also willing to pass on his knowledge and took apprentices, the most famous of whom was Elizabeth Sanderson. She is known to have quilted and designed patterns from around 1880 until near her death in 1934. She in her turn also trained apprentices. It is said that she could mark two quilts a day and only charged 1s for doing so, though Mrs Fox remembers her mother telling her that her grandmother, Mrs Elizabeth Wray of South Hylton, paid 1s 6d for the service at Allenhead before the First World War.

After 1883, people could post quilt tops to Allenheads instead of taking them in person, as the new parcel post had been added to the letter post service. Parcel Post as we know it, run by the government post office, was first instituted in August 1883. To send a 2lb parcel in its early days cost the sum of 6d, then in 1886 the price was lowered to $4\frac{1}{2}$d. It went down yet again in 1897 to 4d where it stayed until 1915, when it went up to 5d, then again in 1918 to 6d. There was obviously inflation during and after the First World War, as in 1920 the price rose again, this time to 9d, but went down again in 1923 to 6d, where it stayed until 1940. The price kept slowly increasing by a penny until it reached the price of 1s 1d in 1953. In 1968 this same parcel cost 3s to send nationally but 2s locally until 1971 when our coinage changed and decimalisation began. In that year a 2lb parcel would cost 21p ordinary parcel and 16p local parcel, but in 1987 the equivalent cost had become £1.50 and £1.30.

The Allenheads style was quite distinctive, with its more freehand approach. Large central motifs spilled into the diamond filling pattern around it and borders sprang from the corners

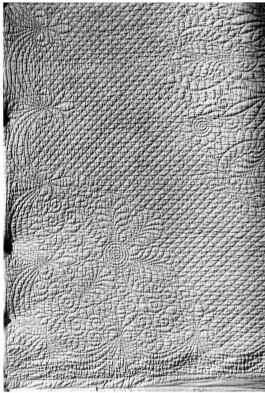

Fig. 46 *Corner of an Allenheads drawn quilt worked by Elizabeth Wray*

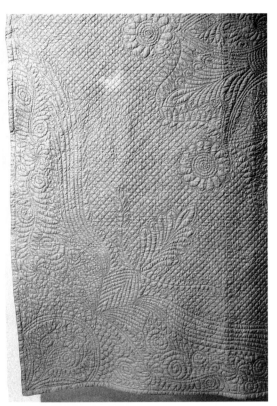

Fig. 47 *Corner of a yellow sateen quilt drawn by Elizabeth Sanderson*

Fig. 48 *Gold quilt drawn by Elizabeth Sanderson*

with a profusion of scrolls, flowers and leaves. Naturally some of these ideas seeped into contemporary work. (See colour plate 8.)

When making patterns there is no need to copy slavishly from old designs or even to use traditional templates, though perhaps they are a good way to start. First take one template and see how many different ways you can make patterns, repeating the shape in straight lines, then using it alternately on the front, then reversed. After that, twist it around and make other different repeats – just keep playing and enjoying yourself. After border patterns, start making motifs, and after that repeat with other templates, finally making patterns with combinations.

If you would like to make your own patterns, look around at what nature has provided. Have you looked at the bud of a horse-chestnut tree when it is opening out, what a marvellous asymmetrical pattern it makes, or an old tree stump?

Fig. 49 *Goosetail patterns*

Fig. 50 *Quarter of a design using the templates Goosewing, Hammock and Rose*

If you live in a city where there are very few trees, other things could give you inspiration, for instance wrought ironwork, windows, or mouldings round walls and doors in old houses. Circles and curved lines make excellent patterns for quilting, so perhaps a look at flowers in the florist's window would be helpful, or weeds along a wall or hedgerow could give you inspiration.

Large quilts are not always wanted on beds nowadays, but are sometimes made as wall hangings. Cot quilts however, are often made when a new baby arrives. The size of these vary from about 20in by 30in (51cm by 77cm) to 30in by 55in (77cm by 140cm), according to the size of the cot and whether or not it is needed to be tucked down under the mattress or just lie on the top.

When making patterns for children, think of what they would like. What would interest them? Perhaps butterflies, a popular book or current televison programme such as Thomas the Tank Engine or Postman Pat. Turn some of these ideas into a picture, with or without a border.

Inspiration for patterns can be taken from many sources, for instance *lettering*. Many different patterns can be derived from this source; not only are there twenty-six letters in our alphabet, but there are many different ways to print, write and draw each one, even if we take only the more rounded letters and make patterns placing them back to back, face to face, repeats with a half drop, etc. etc. Border patterns, all-over patterns and motifs can be made not only for quilts and cushions, but for such things as bags, belts and panels.

Something that has to be thought about in designing a pattern is the area which it has to fill. Is it for a square cushion or a humbug-shaped cushion; is the pattern to cover only the front of a clutch bag or has it to fill the whole rectangle with the front as the most important, or is it to fill part of, or the whole of a waistcoat to wear with a particular dress? Look at the way in which Celtic patterns fill the space. Drawings from this source of inspiration could fill a notebook and supply you with ideas for many things, large and small.

When making a quilt, cushion, bag, waistcoat or anything else, consideration must be given to the size and area to be quilted. The design should fill the whole of the space and not just the centre. The quilting should look designed for that shape. Look at the feather patterns in Fig. 25: see how they fill the various triangles and squares. A good example of how pattern can fill the space provided is demonstrated in the extant uncut Elizabethan slips. In these, the embroidery completely covers a rectangle, filling it with flower patterns. It is just as important for us to learn how designs should fill a given space now as it was in the sixteenth century, though perhaps the reasons are different.

Having made your main pattern, the surrounding area has to be considered. You must be able to 'read' what you have drawn, as it would be a shame if it just disappeared into a sea of bumps. The background, whether plain or patterned, is very important indeed, and so filling patterns, even the simplest, must be well chosen and the correct size considered to make good contrasts.

Fig. 51 *Horse chestnut bud*

CHESTNUT BUD

BORDER PATTERN
PERHAPS FOR A
BELT

Fig. 52 *Patterns based on chestnut bud*

Fig. 53 *An old tree-stump*

Fig. 54 *Georgian window over a door*

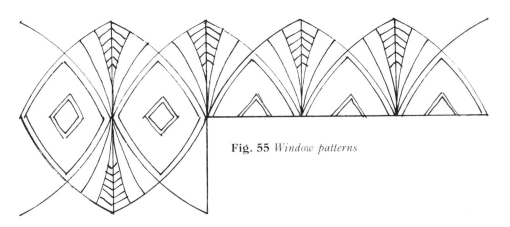

Fig. 55 *Window patterns*

Fig. 56 *Georgian window over a door*

Fig. 57 *Georgian window over a door*

BORDER FROM WINDOW

INSPIRED BY MOULDING AT WALLINGTON HALL

MOTIF FROM WINDOW

Fig. 58 *Window patterns*

Fig. 59 *Sample worked by Lyndon Say prior to making a cot quilt. Fabric dye was used to colour the penguin*

Fig. 60 *Diagram of a cot quilt nearing completion, by the author*

Fig. 61 *Belt in gold lamé designed and made by the
author, with the letter 'a'*

Fig. 62 *Quilted box lid by author in gold kid designed
with the letters GM*

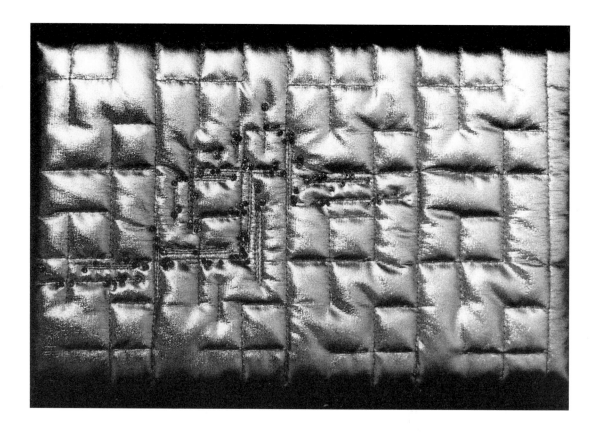

Fig. 63 *Gold lamé evening bag by Ann Hayes, designed with her initials A E H*

Fig. 64 *'Celtic' by Ann Hayes. Quilted in blue shot slub silk*

5
FILLING PATTERNS

Patterns can be beautiful yet not show their beauty. They can be large or small, yet not be distinguishable from their surroundings because they are of a similar size or density. For example, when walking in the greenhouse of a garden centre you may be confronted with hundreds of plants of the same variety, which look absolutely marvellous and a riot of colour, but can you see the beauty and form of a single plant? I suggest not, as only when a plant is lifted away from the others and held against a different background, can true shape be seen. Contrast can also be made the other way round: the background can be small or highly patterned and the object large and smooth.

The most important thing about a pattern is contrast. If your quilting design is not well contrasted, either with a plain background or one with very small pattern, it will just look like a sea of bumps, and apart from the warmth it might give, you may as well have saved your labour. Therefore your background pattern must receive as much consideration as the main one. A question to ask yourself at the drawing stage is, how small has the background to be to make the design look bold? (not, how large to enable me to finish?). It can take longer to work a background than the main pattern, as more stitchery is involved.

When at the designing stage draw the background to scale, repeating with different sizes until you find the correct density and contrast. If it looks correct on paper it will be so when stitched. There is no point in having a beautiful design if it cannot be seen.

Contrast can also be achieved by outlining, but it must be remembered that it takes two lines of stitchery to make one outlined row, three rows of stitchery for two outlines and four rows to make three outlines. Border patterns can be emphasised well with this method, but the rows must be fairly close together or the object will be defeated. The lines should be no more than half an inch apart for a quilt and even closer on smaller items.

There are traditional background or filling patterns, some of which are easier to draw than others. The most popular on old quilts is the diamond, which can be square, elongated, or sloping. Quilters of the past used to have a gauge or stick of the required width, to lay on the fabric and mark against, by drawing with either a needle or chalk. Of course there are variations, such as a double diamond, or plaid patterns, but the quilts made in clubs usually had plain diamonds using a one-inch rule, as time was at such a premium.

The wineglass pattern (made by using a wineglass) can, like other patterns, be of any size. It can be used as a filling to contrast the main pattern, the infill of a large pattern, or, in a large form, as the complete pattern in itself.

Of course you do not have to stay with traditional filling patterns; all you need is an interlocking design, the inspiration for which could come from even a child's toy. Nottingham Museum was where Mrs Carol Atter found her inspiration, when viewing Elizabethan embroidery. She drew and experimented at home to achieve an interlocking pattern for her appliqué and quilted waistcoat.

Filling patterns can be used very successfully as the main pattern on small articles. Focal points are sometimes needed, and these can be

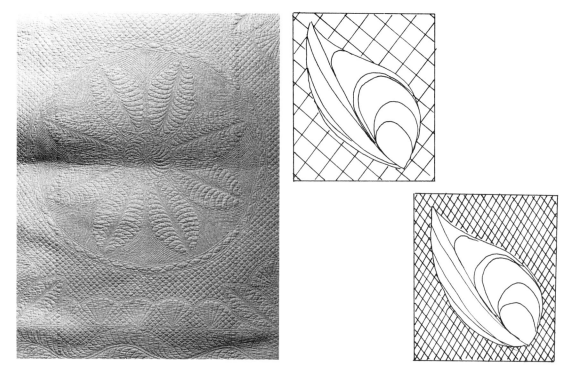

Fig. 65 *Off-white cotton quilt which has a well con-trasted central motif*

Fig. 66 *Bad and good contrast*

Fig. 67 *Border of white quilt,* circa *1920. Four close rows of running stitch make the contrast between wider rows*

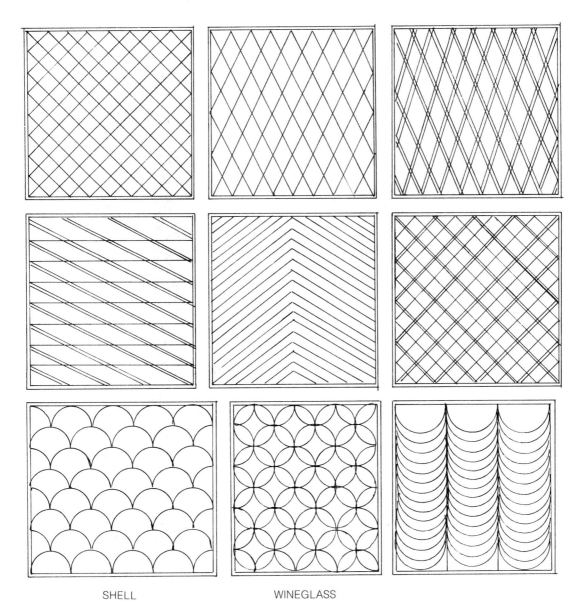

SHELL   WINEGLASS

Fig. 68 *Filling patterns*

created by additional rows of stitching, emphasising the design in the appropriate area and thus making it look richer.

The gold lamé evening bag designed with a simple interlocking cross was quilted with the basic pattern first. To help decide the most suitable place for the focal point, a mock-up with paper told me where the folds should be, the size for this 9 inch wide bag being: front $5\frac{1}{2}$ inches, back $6\frac{1}{2}$ inches, and under the flap 5 inches. These measurements were marked at the sides of the material. The extra lines and half lines were stitched to make a focal point on the back of the bag, repeated on the front, with the addition of small beads and sequins to add a little glitter.

If you wish to use this idea, first draw round your chosen template about 20 times, each in isolation. Fill them all differently with a simple pattern. Then, using the template, draw a number of interlocking areas where you can try one or more of the patterns as repeats.

Take your favourite pattern from the repeats and, starting in the middle of a new area, draw one or three of these. Around them draw some of the filling lines, getting fewer as you near the outside, until they vignette completely into the background. The same pattern can have a number of variations, so try at least two more to give you a choice.

65

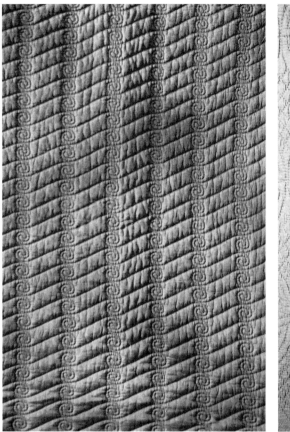

Fig. 69 *Machine-made quilt which gives a contrasting striped effect, although made with rows of continuous lines in a small pattern*

Fig. 70 *Pink quilt with an all-over design using the 'wineglass' pattern*

Fig. 71 *Bag with a variation of the wineglass pattern by Marian Bowman*

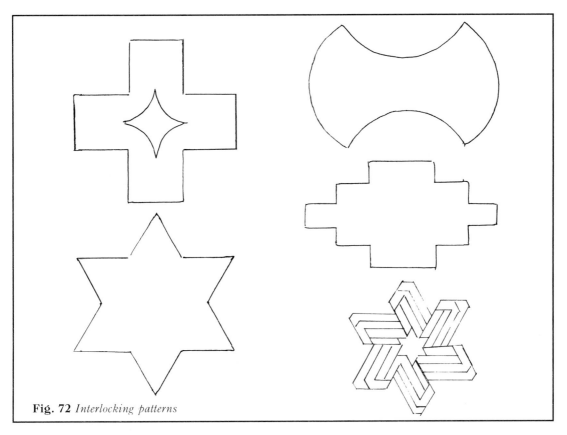

Fig. 72 *Interlocking patterns*

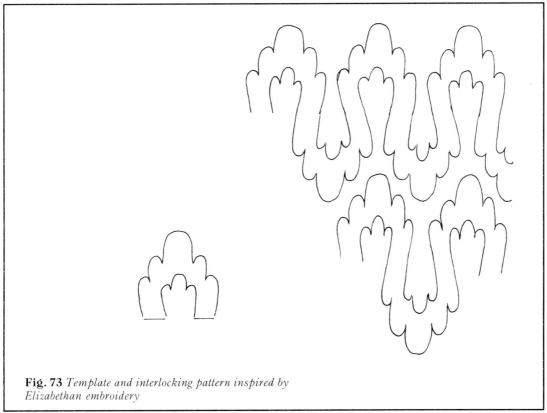

Fig. 73 *Template and interlocking pattern inspired by Elizabethan embroidery*

Fig. 74 *Gold lamé evening bag with an interlocking cross pattern enriched on the front with beads and sequins by the author*

Fig. 75 *A child's building toy was used by the author to make an all-over pattern on the gold lamé evening bag*

Fig. 76 *Shell template patterns*

SHELL TEMPLATE WITH DIFFERENT FILLING PATTERNS

ALL OVER PATTERN USING SHELL TEMPLATE, WITH FILLINGS TO MAKE A FOCAL POINT

Fig. 77 *Clam shell all-over pattern with different fillings*

6
FASHION, ACCESSORIES AND PANELS

Whether we like it or not, fashion plays a large part in our lives, affecting our purchases of clothes, food, accessories and equipment. The clothing industry is the best example of ever-changing trends, with quilted garments going in and out of fashion, and hemlines, loose and tight-fitting clothes varying in popularity as the years go by. At the moment, padded articles of clothing are very popular, with the anorak, ski clothes, and some long coats as prime examples of the commercial wadded quilting technique. These clothes often differ in warmth according to the amount of filling used.

Quilted motifs which may be applied to lighter types of clothing, such as jumpers, sweaters and blouses, are in vogue at the moment and the quilted waistcoat comes and goes in high fashion, but still seems to remain popular. These commercial items seldom follow any traditional quilting pattern; the embroid-erer, when wanting an individual waistcoat, usually finds a design from something that interests her.

The waistcoat by Mrs Ann Kinnement, which could be called *Autumn Leaves*, was inspired by her Australian vine houseplant. The material is natural noille silk, which she says was lovely to work with and also beautiful to wear. For her design she took a few leaves and stuck them to the silk with double-sided sellotape (to act as templates), then sprayed with fabric dye. After taking the leaves off she used them again to print, painting the backs with fabric dye and changing the colours as required. The quilting stitches run round some of the leaves and round the outline that the printed pattern made. The shape created is repeated on the rest of the

waistcoat and machined to hold the three layers in place.

Another waistcoat, made by Mrs Lyndon Say from cream polyester crepe lined with polyester cotton and filled with 3oz polyester wadding, was inspired by one of her husband's photo-graphs of a double arc rainbow with reflections (which is why there are two rainbows in one direction and a third in the other, so I am told).

A jacket, also made by Mrs Lyndon Say, used Weardale for her inspiration. At the bottom she has used a Weardale Chain, from which grow the stems of plants and grasses, and the aubretia flower-shapes above represent her garden. The material is polyester cotton on both sides and she used 4oz polyester wadding for the filling. Once again, traditional running stitches are used in the quilting, and I am told that it washes beautifully in her domestic washing machine.

As I said in chapter 4, when designing for such an item as a waistcoat one must consider the shape of the garment, as the pattern needs to be an integral part of the shape. First doodle many outlines with various fillings to get the feel of the article. It could be that you already have a favourite waistcoat pattern, or you could sim-ply cut some paper and fit it to you. In either case try out different lengths, or necklines, but whatever you do, make the embroidery fit the shape to make a united whole.

Other articles of clothing can be treated the same way. An evening skirt for instance, where either the hem or the whole dress could be quilted. It could be in any style, such as the wrap-over style which is both fashionable and practical.

Fig. 78 *Natural noille silk quilted waistcoat by Ann Kinnement*

Fig. 79 *Rainbow bolero by Lyndon Say*

Fig. 80 *Back of rainbow bolero by Lyndon Say*

Fig. 81 *Jade green quilted jacket, 'Weardale' by Lyndon Say*

WAISTCOAT DOODLES

SKIRT DOODLES

Fig. 82 *Waistcoat and skirt doodles*

Accessories

A belt and a clutch bag have already been mentioned in chapter 4 (see belt photo page 61), but there are other shapes which would be interesting to make. Sock-slippers for cosy evenings around the fire, or gloves with quilted backs, can be fun to make.

Various embroidery methods can be used in conjunction with quilting – for instance, beading, goldwork, surface stitchery and dyes. With small amounts of fabric dye becoming accessible to the layman, new fields have opened up to the embroiderer. Quilting is quite a subtle medium and, therefore, when mixing one form with another one has to be careful. Very strong contrasting colours do not show off quilting, so care must be taken when using these if it is to be the quilting which is of the major importance.

Subtle colour changes can be used to great effect and can be achieved with very fine chiffon. The finest I have found is in chiffon scarves. A piece is laid over the whole of the area to be quilted and the stitches worked through all the layers. After completion the unwanted chiffon is cut away at the stitched line. This does not pull off the top when on panels, as here there is no wear and tear, but this method is not suitable for use on clothing.

Panels

The inspiration for pieces of work to hang on walls can come from nature just as the traditional quilting templates did. Nature has such a wealth of pattern and design to offer, ready for us to treat in endless ways. If you give the subject 'trees' to a number of people, each will conjure up something very different. One person might think of a solitary tree in leaf, another the overall structure and grandure, another the bark. Others might think of a copse or row of trees, or a wood, or trees in blossom, or the variations of leaves from different trees. One such panel is of a tree beside a small stream, worked by Mrs Wyn Bacon; another by the author uses the foliage for the quilted background with a free-standing branch of leaves and apples.

The materials used for these panels varies. The panel called 'Leaves in Spring Sunshine' by Mrs Sheila Corfe is worked on calico, using fabric dye crayons to add delicate colour. 'Golden Apples' uses gold transfer print lamé overlaid with a very thin blue chiffon for the back-

Fig. 83 *Quilted and beaded gold lamé neckpiece to be worn on a black dress or jumper, made by the author*

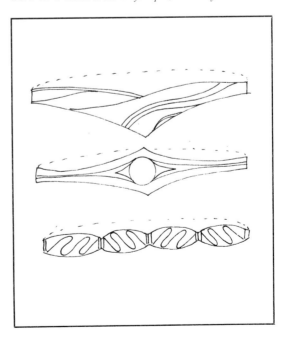

Fig. 84 *Ideas for belts*

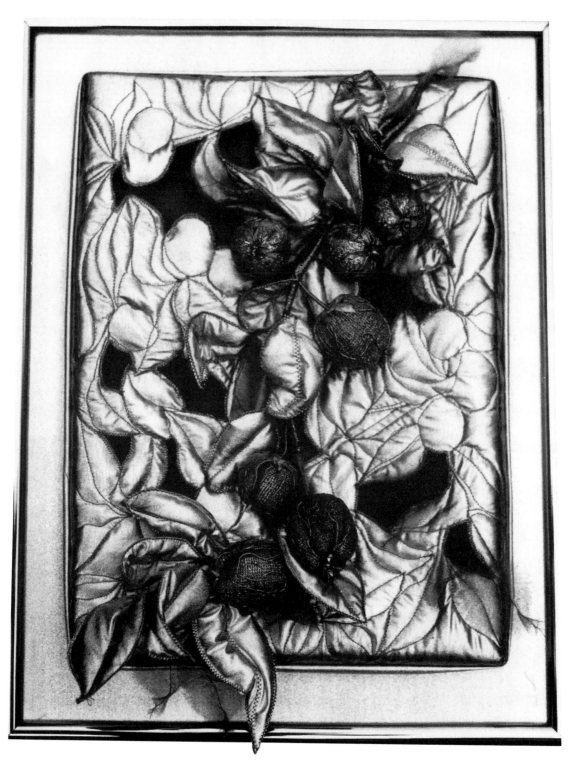

Fig. 85 *'Golden Apples' by the author. Embroidery in three layers, the middle being quilted foliage in gold lamé*

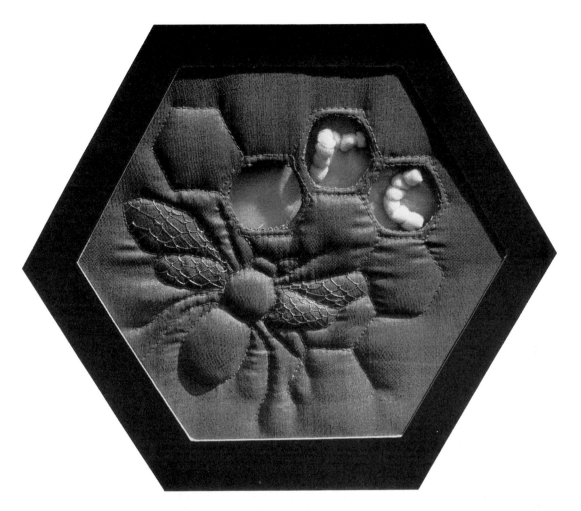

Fig. 86 *'Honeycomb' by Sandra Felce in pink silk*

ground, while 'Down By The Stream' by the author and Wyn Bacon and 'Celtic' by Mrs Ann Hayes use shot tussah silk. 'The Honeycombe' by Mrs Sandra Felce is worked on Honan silk.

Bronze kid was quilted for the panel 'Stone Bronze', the design of which was based upon a wall which interested the author when on holiday. This raised effect is very pronounced, but only because of the shine and inherant quality of the kid. Gold kid was also used for the box lid designed with letters **g.m.** on page 61.

Quilting can be used to make small articles such as boxes or greetings cards. Perhaps a special card shaped like a key for a twenty-first birthday. The one worked by the author for her daughter incorporates her name in the top roundel of the handle. It exploits the play of light and shade made on round patterns on the shiny gold transfer print lamé.

As can be seen, quilting blends quite well with other types of embroidery to give a raised surface or to add a softness which possibly cannot be achieved in any other way.

Fig. 87 *'Down by the Stream', worked by Wyn Bacon.*
Seeding is used to contrast the tree and copper threads
complement the colour of the shot silk

Fig. 88 *'Leaves in Spring Sunshine' by Shiela Corfe is worked in calico*

Fig. 89 *'Stone Bronze' by the author is quilted bronze kid*

Fig. 90 *A 21st birthday card in gold lamé, by the author*

Fig. 91 *A Christmas card, machine quilted in silver lamé, by the author*

7
METHODS AND MATERIALS

Materials

The materials used for quilted bedding have varied only slightly through the centuries. Three layers of fabric are still needed; a back, a fluffy middle and a top layer. Fashion has varied the outside fabrics from silk and satin through furnishing fabrics and cotton prints to cotton sateen and, since the Second World War, to man-made fibres such as polyester crepe or satin and mixtures of man-made and natural fibres like polyester cotton.

Quilted leather for body armour was used in the days before the pistol was invented to protect against arm to arm combat and hand-flung weapons. Under metal armour, quilted garments of linen or wool were worn to prevent chaffing. Later, when the early American settlers needed protection against Indian arrows, they made quilted leather jackets, waistcoats and short tunics.

Filling. The middle layer of fabric, which in America is called *batting*, was, until the last war, made of natural fibres, varying according to circumstances. Since the war the man-made fibres produced have included nylon, Terylene and now polyester wadding.

In the past, cotton wadding was the most commonly used filling in this area, though in some quilts wool fleece has been found. Worn blankets and clothing such as men's wool vests and 'long johns' were sometimes used as they were very economical. The garments were cut, flattened out and interleaved to create an even layer. Very occasionally, paper wadding was used, which must have been much cheaper than the 'cotton wool', but very unsatisfactory, as it

was less easy to stitch through and had a disastrous effect when washed, as it impacts on the first washing to become very heavy and almost board-like.

Cotton wadding was bought by weight in large rolls. The wadding was packed as tightly as possible to minimise the size. When the roll was opened and unfolded it needed to be placed in a warm atmosphere and left to expand. This 'cotton wool' could be purchased in haberdashery stores at the same time as buying other materials. There were different qualities, but one which was often used still had the husks of cotton-seed among the fibres. These husks were hard and often made a quilter's finger very sore when she was working.

With the advent of man-made fibres, cotton wadding was used less and less. Terylene wadding came on the market, but was rather stiff when quilted, and has now been superseded by polyester. This wadding comes in different thicknesses, 2oz, 3oz, 4oz and 8oz being the usual for quilting. There is though, a much heavier weight for furnishings. Polyester wadding can vary slightly. I find that some types are more matted and harder than others and it is advisable, therefore, when needing wadding, to consider whether you would prefer the softer variety, which can be teased apart, or the firmer, stiffer type.

Cotton wadding had to be held down at regular intervals as the fibres could move; the rule was that it had to be stitched every inch. If you look at a well-washed and worn quilt, the reason for this will become plain. When wool was used it had to be spread evenly over the back material as it did not come in large sheet form. These fibres, which did not move like cotton, were resilient and light in weight, but nevertheless the quilting was just as closely patterned.

Domette is a fluffy, knitted material that is sometimes used as the filling, giving a thin and plyable layer.

The back material. Of matching or contrasting colour, this is, nowadays, usually the same as the front. In the past sometimes a heavier fabric, occasionally patterned and often bearing no relation to the front, was used, availability, necessity and sheer practicality being deciding factors.

Quantity. The amount of material needed to make a quilt was 7½ yards in length for both top and bottom layer, plus the equivalent in wadding. Material is taken up by the quilting and so when estimating for small articles one inch is allowed, two inches are added for a thin quilt, and three inches for a thicker one. Seam allowances also have to be taken into consideration when planning the exact size.

In the early 1900s the cotton sateen that seemed to be preferred by quilters was 'Silver Sheen'. One or two people have told me that it did not fade, was of good quality and easy to work. Mrs Horan bought hers at Robinsons in Lynch Street, Hartlepool, while Mrs Pickering shopped at Binns in Fawcett Street, Sunderland. This material is not available now, much to the disgust of some older quilters.

Thread. The thread used for stitching must be strong. Quilters in the past would not use a mercerised thread, as they said it was not strong enough, preferring a 40 sewing cotton or stronger yarn. When flat quilting was popular for coverlets in the eighteenth century, silk thread, such as buttonhole twist, and linen threads were used. Nowadays special quilting threads can be bought. Natural fibres are preferred to a polyester core and cotton surround. The old maxim is, 'cotton thread for a cotton fabric, silk thread for a silk fabric and a man-made thread for a man-made fabric'. The important thing about the thread is that it must be both strong and suitable for the article you are making.

Needles. Usually 'betweens' numbers, 7, 8, or 9, are the best, according to the thickness of thread being used. These needles are shorter than sharps or crewel needles and excellent when sewing with a thimble, being just the right length for comfort. However if you are a person who does not use a thimble a longer needle, such as a crewel or sharps, will be better, and will enable you to draw the needle through.

Methods

Transferring the design. *Scoring* the fabric is the traditional way to transfer a design. Take a thick needle with a large eye, such as a no. 16 chenille needle, and thread with a short length of thick yarn. This allows the needle to be held with ease. Keeping the needle as level with the surface of the material as possible, press down with the thumb and draw round the template. In this way a scored line is achieved which does not scratch or damage the material. This method is only satisfactory on natural fibres such as silk and cotton, where the impression will remain long enough for the quilting to be finished. Man-made fibres, such as polyester, dacron or nylon, will not hold a scored line for long, so marking in some other way is necessary.

Water-soluble fabric marker pens are useful on poly-cotton materials, but totally man-made fabrics have a solid filament which is not able to hold a clear line, as it spreads and sometimes runs until it becomes unreadable. To obliterate any marks, cold water has to be used. The best results seem to be obtained when cold water is allowed to run through the whole of the fabric, for example under a shower. If only wetted on the line, a water mark or bleeding effect sometimes results. Do not use hot water or put the article in the washer with detergent, as you may be left with a yellow stain.

Water-soluble crayons such as Cumberland Derwent colour, or Caran d'âche, can, if kept to a sharp point, be used for synthetic fabrics or for someone whose sight is not good enough to see a scored line. Keep the colour as close to the shade of fabric as possible. Your stitching should cover up the line and there will be no need to wash the article, though if this is done any colour will come out.

A light table or a window is useful when transferring the design for a small article such as a cushion or a panel. Not many people have light tables but there is nearly always a window in the room. Stick your design, preferably drawn on tracing paper, on to the window pane, possibly with sellotape. Then stick your carefully ironed fabric over the top, hold it firm and still, and, using your water-soluble crayon, trace the pattern. The design can be seen more easily when the sun is shining, and the thickness of the fabric will also have some bearing as to how clearly you can see the tracing, but most fabrics can be used this way. White crayon on white fabric has been used with success, which shows that a strong colour is not neccessary. Perhaps it would be best to keep to a colour just one or two shades darker than the material.

Preparation. Material must be prepared before using, even though this might only mean ironing to get all the crease marks out and then marking out the design. When making a large quilt the fabric is usually narrower than the finished quilt width and must be joined. Avoid making a seam down the middle. Use one length for a central panel, dividing the other length in two in order to make seams either side. These lengths are best joined by hand-stitching to keep the tension of the quilt constant. A great number of old quilts, particularly those from quilt clubs, were machine-stitched for speed, but this does not mean that we should emulate them.

Guidelines are often tacked or marked on to a large quilt top before drawing in order to keep the pattern straight. If the whole design is marked before starting to stitch, it is done prior to dressing the frame, but if marked whilst working then guidelines must be done first.

The back layer of material, whether for a quilt, a waistcoat or a panel, is stretched on a frame. The tightness of this will depend upon the article to be quilted. A panel, where the back is not seen, needs to be very tight, in order to allow all the moulding caused by the stitchery to show on the front. For reversible articles, the back material is kept taut but not tight.

Dressing a frame for a quilt. Stitch the backing material to the webbing on both the stretcher bars, and tightly roll all but 18 inches of it round the back stretcher. Peg the slats in place to keep the material taut, but not tight.

The wadding is now placed over the backing with the front edge pinned to the front stretcher, the surplus being left to hang over the back stretcher. The top material is treated in the same manner. The three edges on the front are now sewn together. The materials hanging over the back of the frame act as a weight and give tension. They may be loosely and neatly folded into a dust sheet and held off the floor. The surplus wadding and top material must not be rolled round the top stretcher like the backing; as some of this will be taken up with the

stitchery, and so must be left free to move.

After the three layers are put together the sides are taped round the slats to complete the tension and to keep the materials from moving. A good quality tape, about $\frac{3}{8}$ inch to 1 inch in width, is preferable, as it can be used many times, also good quality steel pins which should not rust. The tape is pinned through all three layers starting at the side edge near the front stretcher, then taken over the side slat to the back and pinned in a likewise manner, repeating back and forth until reaching the top. This process is repeated on the other side. The frame should now be taut, but not tight as there must be enough movement in the fabric to allow the needle to pass through almost vertically.

Only about 18 inches of the design should be visible on the frame at any one time, and the hands must be able to reach the design easily without stretching. The stitching is usually started at the bottom right-hand side and worked across the frame.

Where the design continues into the unseen part, the needle and thread are left on the line until the quilt is 'rolled on'. They are then ready to continue without any joinings. This is why as many as 50 needles were threaded ready for the quilters of the past.

When all the design that can be seen is stitched, the tapes are taken off, the slats removed and the stitched part rolled on to the front stretcher. The back stretcher is unrolled for 18 inches, and the slats and tape are then returned, ready to quilt once again. It is advisable to cover up the stitching with a dust sheet so that it does not get snagged or dirty.

Stitching. A *running stitch* is the traditional method of working. This sounds quite easy but the stitch and the space should be equal on both sides. This gives a broken line, but makes it possible to create a reversible article.

To achieve good stitches, put the needle in the fabric as near vertical as possible, keeping the other hand underneath. When the needle touches the finger, push the needle back to the right side, also making it vertical. This is helped by the top hand depressing the material behind the needle slightly. At least three stitches should be made before drawing the thread through. It takes quite a lot of practice to achieve this rocking motion and be able to make a few even stitches at one time, so beginners are perhaps best advised to make only one or two stitches until they feel more confident.

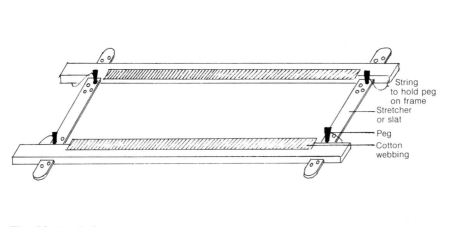

Fig. 92 *A quilt frame*

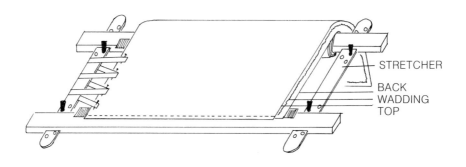

Fig. 93 *A dressed frame with the taping not yet repeated over the other stretcher*

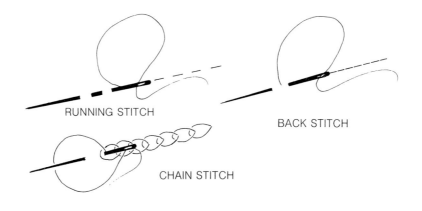

Fig. 94 *Stitches*

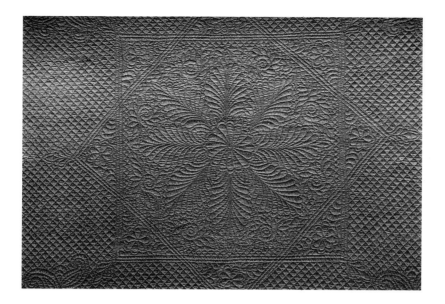

Fig. 95 *Central panel of a fine white quilt*

When it is not necessary for an article to be reversible, other stitches may be used. The *back stitch* gives an unbroken line and therefore better definition, and is used quite often and for quilting on panels. Another useful stitch is *chain stitch*, which also gives an unbroken line but thicker than the last. If worked well the back will look like a back stitch, and it could therefore be used on a reversible article.

To start stitching, make a small knot. Insert the needle on the stitching line a little from the starting point and make a stitch through the top material and filling only, bringing the needle up at the beginning of the line. Give a gentle sharp tug to pull the knot through and embed it in the wadding. Proceed to stitch. To finish, work a back stitch on the wrong side and bring the needle diagonally through the wadding to the top, then snip the thread.

Washing. Quilts have been found to wash very satisfactorily in a domestic washing machine and in fact retain a clearer colour than when dry cleaned – they were, after all, made with the rigours of poss-tubs in mind. It is perhaps better after spinning to dry them flat, possibly on a blanket spread over a carpeted floor or outside. If hung on a clothes-line, a strain is put on the quilting which does not give such good results. However a tumble-drier gives the best drying results as the warmth and tumbling action fluff up the filling attractively. Before any wetting of quilts, colour fastness must be checked first.

8
FINISHINGS

Once the quilting or embroidery is completed, do not make the mistake of thinking that your work is done – it must now be presented. Whether it is a cushion or quilt to finish, a panel to lace or a skirt to make, the finish can make or break it.

A quilt or cushion has at least three different ways which it could be made up; with a piped, bound, or turned in edge. A panel needs to be mounted and there are at least two different ways to stretch your work over hardboard or card, with at least five different ways of presenting the finished piece.

Quilts

Turned-in hem. The majority of traditional quilts have the edges of both the back and front material turned in and stitched, either with running stitches or by machine (this being the quickest way), which was of paramount importance when running a quilt club.

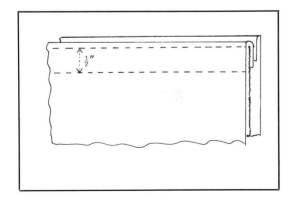

Fig. 96 *Turned hem with two rows of running stitches*

Piped edge. Made with crossway strips, this is a good way to finish a quilt. It gives a strong, firm edge, as it is thicker than the quilt and so takes most of the 'wear'. It can also be unpicked and replaced when it gets shabby without altering the rest of the quilt, unlike a worn turned-in hem, which can only be bound or cut off and turned again.

Bound edge. This needs the material at one side to be slightly larger than the other, which is then folded over the raw edges and blind hemmed. Alternatively, crossway strips can be used, stitched down first on the front with a running or back stitch, pressed open, and blind hemmed on the back after turning in a hem.

Mounting panels

When the embroidery has been completed and taken off the frame, it needs stretching over hardboard or card. Card does not have to be extremely thick, as two thinner pieces glued together can make quite a rigid backing if stuck with the grain of each in opposite directions. There are two methods of mounting; lacing or gluing calico on to the board.

Method 1: Lacing
1 Cut and prepare the board. Cut a piece of thin polyester wadding or some other type of padding, such as felt, domette or foam, to the size of the board. This may be anchored at the edges with a tiny dot of glue, just enough to hold it whilst putting the embroidery over the top. This padding hardly shows when the material is finally pulled tight, but it does absorb any lumps and thick threads that have been taken

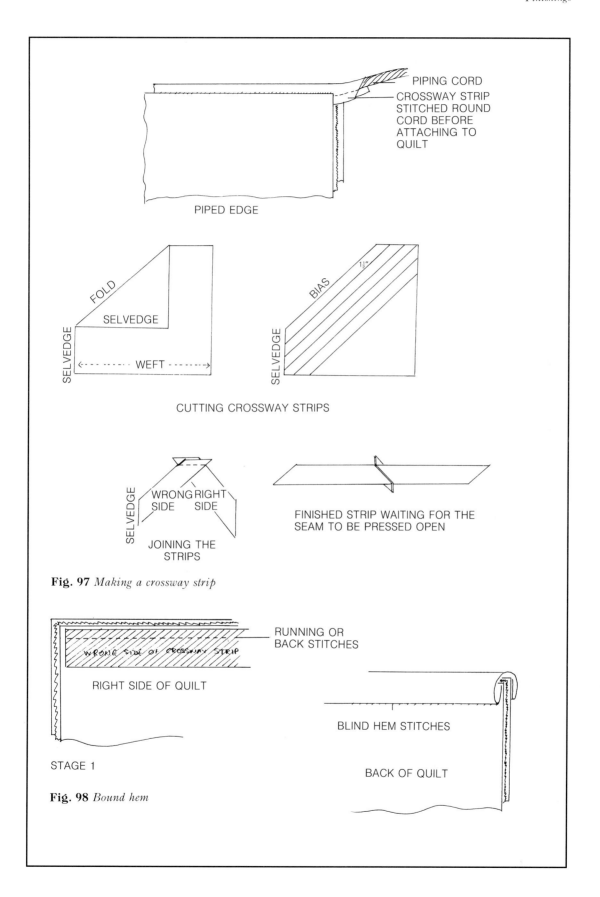

PIPING CORD

CROSSWAY STRIP STITCHED ROUND CORD BEFORE ATTACHING TO QUILT

PIPED EDGE

FOLD

SELVEDGE

SELVEDGE

WEFT

BIAS

1¾"

SELVEDGE

CUTTING CROSSWAY STRIPS

SELVEDGE

WRONG SIDE RIGHT SIDE

JOINING THE STRIPS

FINISHED STRIP WAITING FOR THE SEAM TO BE PRESSED OPEN

Fig. 97 *Making a crossway strip*

RUNNING OR BACK STITCHES

WRONG SIDE OF CROSSWAY STRIP

RIGHT SIDE OF QUILT

STAGE 1

Fig. 98 *Bound hem*

BLIND HEM STITCHES

BACK OF QUILT

through to the back. It also gives a better finish.

2 Place your embroidery over the board, making sure that the grain of the material is straight at the sides and that the embroidery is centred.

3 Pin into the edge of the card or hardboard. Check to see the embroidery is in the correct place.

4 Take a ball of very thin, strong string and thread a needle with one end. Do not cut off a length.

5 Starting just away from one corner, make a diagonal stitch.

6 Make another stitch on the opposite side of the card.

7 Continue making diagonal stitches on alternate sides, but each time vary the distance from the edge of the material. This is to vary the 'pull' on the fabric so that it will not shread.

8 At the end, fasten off the string with two or three back stitches.

9 Tighten the lacing-up back on to the ball. Leaving just a few inches of string, cut enough to thread a needle and fasten off after making sure that the embroidery is tight. Before finally fastening off, check that the embroidery is placed centrally and that the grain has not been disturbed in the tightening process.

10 At the corners a slice can be cut off the back material if there is one, but the top material is folded as neatly and flatly as possible. It is not possible to do a proper mitre, because of the thickness of the board, but the material should be folded in a similar fashion.

11 Lace up the second side like the first, and remove the pins.

12 Draw the lacing tight, winding the string back on to the ball.

13 Fasten off the ends of string.

14 Oversew the corners to keep flat, making sure they are tight.

Method 2: Glueing

1 Prepare your card or hardboard and cut to size.

2 Take some reasonably strong calico (medium weight is sufficient) or other material and cut all round, one inch larger than the board.

3 Place the fabric over the front of the card, making sure the grain is straight, and pin into the edge of the board.

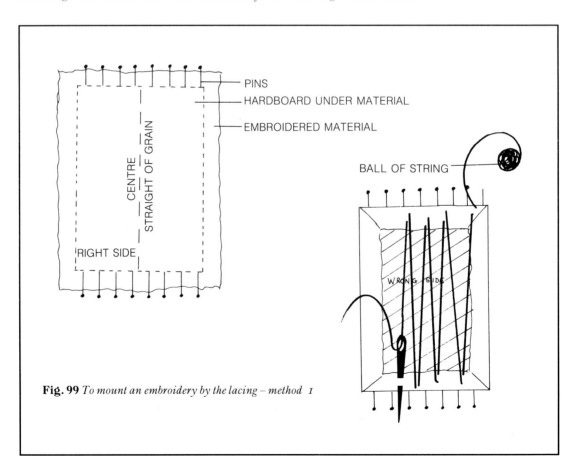

Fig. 99 *To mount an embroidery by the lacing – method* 1

4 On the reverse put a line of glue about half an inch from the edge and stick the calico down, pulling to keep tight. It is important not to let the glue seep to the edge of the board.

5 The pins may be removed.

6 If you wish, use a thin layer of wadding, the exact size of the board, as in Method 1.

7 The embroidery is laid over the wadding and calico, keeping the grain straight and embroidery central. Pin into the edge of the card, making sure that the embroidery is taut.

8 Turn to the back and, using a curved needle, stitch the embroidery to the calico with small herringbone stitches.

9 Neaten the corners as for Method 1 above, without cutting away any material.

10 Once all four sides are stitched, take another piece of calico, about the same size as the board, turn in a hem and pin to the back.

11 Hem the backing through both layers of fabric.

Presenting panels

Once you have mounted your embroidery, it can be finished and presented. Here are a few suggestions:–

1 Take it to a picture framer, choose a frame and ask him to make it, either with or without glass.

2 A *card mount* within the frame might enhance your embroidery. When this is to be done, decide upon the size of mount needed and cut the hardboard (or card) to those measurements. If you have mounted your work not realising that you would like to use card, it is possible for the framer to pack the back in order to stop the embroidery moving in the frame.

Card (mounting board) comes in various colours and at least two thicknesses, and can be purchased from stationers and art shops. Take your embroidery with you to choose the shade which looks best with your work. Don't guess or leave it to chance.

Always use a knife (craft or Stanley) and a metal-edged ruler when cutting. When you have cut the outside edge, draw on the back, marking the centre down the length and again along the width of the card. It is then easier to centralise the hole to be cut out of the middle.

If the card is cut before the 'lacing' has been done it can be used to make sure that the embroidery is central and has not been accidently pulled to one side.

The alternative to making your own card mount is to ask the picture framer to do this before he frames the panel. He should have the right equipment for this job, and also be able to make a bevelled edge to the card. Make sure that he knows which is the top of the work.

3 A *material frame*. Instead of card, material can be used and often looks more in keeping with the embroidery. With shot materials, you can play on the two colours by making a frame with the warp and weft in the opposite direction to that of the embroidered material. If sewing on a plain background fabric, this could also be used for the frame. A little fabric dye may also be painted on to extend the embroidery into the frame, or a related fabric used to enhance the embroidery. There are other possibilities, which include use of an unusual shape. The main idea is to enhance the embroidery and present it in as beautiful a way as possible. There are at least two ways of making a material frame.

Method 1

1 Glue two pieces of card together (as described earlier in the chapter). Cut out the frame to the required size.

2 Cover one side of the frame with thin polyester wadding, domette, felt or some other material to give it a slightly padded look.

3 Take the material to be used as a covering and cut it one inch larger than the frame on all sides.

4 With the wrong side of the material facing, lay the frame on the top with the padding facing down and cut a small diagonal cross in the centre to give you a start.

5 Work on one inner edge at a time, extending the diagonal line as required.

6 Put a little glue on the card frame and fold back the material. Press in place by stroking it horizontally along the frame to stretch it as tight as possible in that direction and to keep the grain straight. Only cut closely into the second corner after you have done this, as material will usually stretch.

7 Be careful not to cut too far into the corners, but yet far enough so that there will be no puckering when completed.

8 Repeat on the other three sides.

9 To make sure that the corners are 'square' take a thin needle and put a little glue on the end. Carefully transfer this glue to the corner of the card on its thickness, then after cleaning the needle draw it from front to back over the material pressing it into the corner. This will hold it tight and also prevent fraying.

10 Having completed the inner part of the frame, the outer edge is treated in a similar manner, pulling the material taut.

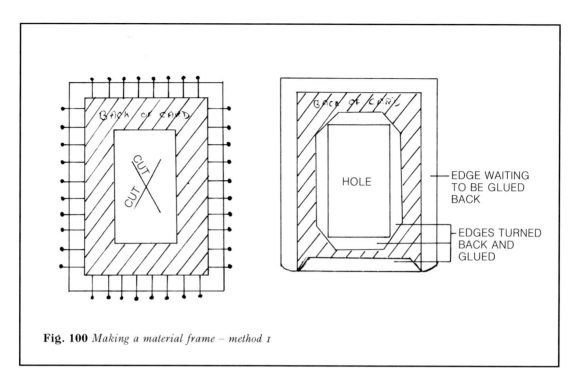

Fig. 100 *Making a material frame – method 1*

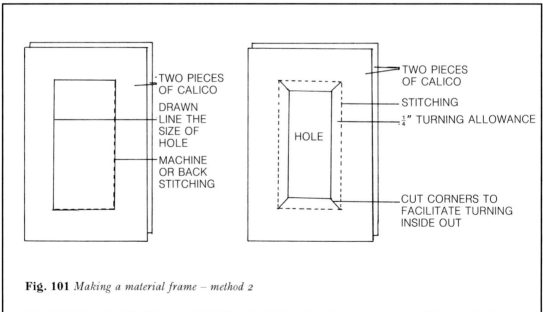

Fig. 101 *Making a material frame – method 2*

11 The frame now can be placed over the embroidery and an outside metal or moulded frame made.

Method 2
This can involve using the sewing machine, or it may be stitched by hand.
1 Cut the frame as before.
2 Cut two pieces of material which are about one inch larger than the frame.

3 Place the frame on the ironed fabric and draw a line round the inside edge.
4 Not forgetting that a line has a thickness, sew (on the machine or using a back stitch) on the edge of the line towards the middle.
5 Cut out the centre hole, leaving about $\frac{1}{4}$ inch turning and nicking the corners.
6 Turn inside out and press.

7 Put any required padding on to the card and place your material round the frame.

8 Keep the stitched inner edge straight, possibly by holding with pins whilst the outer edge is pulled tight and again held with pins along the edge of the card.

9 Glue down the material on the back of the card.

10 Pull the backing material tight and glue or stitch to the front material.

11 Remove the pins.

Double mount or block mount. Another way to present an embroidery after the initial mounting is to take another piece of board and cover it with a matching or contrasting material. This time do not use any padding; apart from this, mount in the same way as the embroidery. The embroidery is then stuck on to this, or tied through previously made holes.

Suppliers

Templates   Durham County Federation of Women's Institutes, 51/2 Crossgate, Durham DH1 4PY

Patterns   (Either traditional or contemporary, for quilts, pillows or cushions. Stamping on request.) Durham Designs, 5 Beresford Park, Sunderland, Tyne & Wear, SR2 7JT

Further reading

M. Fitzrandolph and F.M. Fletcher *Quilting* Dryad Press Ltd
Dorothy Osler *Traditional British Quilts* B.T. Batsford
Averil Colby *Quilting* B.T. Batsford
Averil Colby *Patchwork Quilts* B.T. Batsford
M. Fitzrandolph *Traditional Quilting* B.T. Batsford
Gill Vickers *New Designs in Quilting* Dryad Press Ltd
Florence Peto *American Quilts and Coverlets* Max Parrish & Co. Ltd
Short *Quilting Design, Techniques & Application* B.T. Batsford
Victoria & Albert Museum *Notes on Quilting* HMSO

Index